"In this work, Kennedy gives timely insight into what the 'new sexuality' does and does not mean. We can be fooled by many modern 'experts,' the author tells us, who would have us believe the new myths that swinging is a sign of maturity and freedom, that group sex is a healthy outlet in pursuit of sexual variety, and that masturbation and homosexuality are unequivocally healthy and most desirable expressions of the mature personality. It is the author's contention that the sexual revolution is tremendously overrated, precisely because so many authors have mistaken pseudo and often sensationalistic responses to human searchings for the roots and causes of revolutionary liberation.

Eugene Kennedy, as is his custom, calls us back to reality, by restoring common sense and a deeply Christian perspective to this important area of human relationship. While accepting and rejoicing in the demise of the Puritanical myths of yesteryear, he is adept in pointing out the inconsistencies and dangers of many of the new sexual myths as well. Real human sexuality is more than a neurotic pursuit of the simultaneous orgasm or a blurring of male and female identities. It is on deeper levels that our answers will be found, because it is on deeper levels that human beings are struggling. Here is an author, in an insightful and well-documented book, who appreciates that struggle, who puts his finger on the *real* issues, and helps us to understand them."

—*Best Sellers*

THE NEW SEXUALITY

Books by Eugene C. Kennedy

COMFORT MY PEOPLE
FASHION ME A PEOPLE
THE GENIUS OF THE APOSTOLATE (*with Paul F. D'Arcy*)
IN THE SPIRIT, IN THE FLESH
THE NEW SEXUALITY: *Myths, Fables, and Hang-ups*
THE PAIN OF BEING HUMAN
THE PEOPLE ARE THE CHURCH
THE RETURN TO MAN
A TIME FOR LOVE
WHAT A MODERN CATHOLIC BELIEVES ABOUT SEX
WHAT A MODERN CATHOLIC BELIEVES ABOUT MARRIAGE

THE NEW SEXUALITY

Myths, Fables, and Hang-ups

EUGENE C. KENNEDY

IMAGE BOOKS

A Division of Doubleday & Company, Inc.
Garden City, New York

Image Books Edition
by special arrangement with Doubleday & Company, Inc.
Image Books Edition published September 1973

ISBN: 0-385-06357-1

CONTENTS

INTRODUCTION

This book is intended as a limited survey of the current mythology of human sexual behavior and it has two purposes: First, to note and document the fresh crop of myths that, like a second-generation strain of bacteria, has brought new and more wildly pulsing fevers to contemporary man; secondly, to offer some support and encouragement to the average man of sensibility who, in trying his best to understand and live with and through his sexuality, is often intimidated by the new mythmakers who cause him to feel—if, for example, he has no taste for orgies and still loves the woman he married—hopelessly out of it.

To achieve this goal, I have reviewed both the social commentary and the scientific evidence which we now possess about human sexuality. While it is obvious that not everything can be covered in textbook depth in a work such as this, I believe that the material offered returns an indictment of some of the favorite tenets of the new sexuality. It is actually quite astounding to learn, after a close examination of the literature, how many of the current sexual myths are unrelated to or unsubstantiated by the solid sexual research of recent years. Indeed, it is a refreshing experience to read carefully the work of men and women who, far from fomenting a sexual revolution, attempt calmly to shed light where there has been so much darkness. It is in the spirit of their work, keenly aware of the fact that we are only at the edges of knowledge and the beginnings of wisdom about human sexuality, that the modern myths and hang-ups about sexuality are explored.

I am not doing this, of course, only as a social scientist, but as a human observer whose Christian values about man and life lead me to speak for man's present dignity and still potential destiny. Man is better than the image of him used by the modern sexual mythmakers; he is not a machine in search of the right sexual program nor a totally indifferent agent and receptor of erotic impulses. Man's present difficulties about his sexuality are testimony to the fact that it has not been fully integrated into his personality. The contention of this book is that the present shallow sexual mythology, fascistic and demanding obedience from all, only makes that process of integration more difficult. Simply stated, as it is in a later chapter, you do not cure disintegrated sex by more doses of disintegrated sex. But that is what the new myths amount to: forces that wrench sexuality still further out of its human context and distort and cripple man in the process.

We live in a strange, pendulum-swing world, and we are as far out of balance with some of the new "liberating" myths as we were with the old constraining ones. This book is not an attempt to restore an era in which repression merely forced the expression of sexuality into darkened conduits of behavior while it spoke publicly and hypocritically about purity. Morality has had a bad name because of the immoral rigidities of previous generations whose own myths led them to misemphasize sexuality so badly. Religion—not real religion, but the superficial magic that swelled on the fundamentalistic control of man—has also had a bad name in the area of sexuality. That does not diminish the potential of serious moralists and genuine religion as helpers to man in the task of integrating his sexuality at the present time. Indeed, sexuality is ultimately a religious problem in the authentic sense that it becomes imbued with meaning only in terms of an explanatory system which transcends but interprets man to himself. Too many churchmen think that a return to morality means going back to the days when they could complacently control human behavior at a comfortable distance. They were a clever lot, however, because they understood man's vulnerabilities and they knew that if they could control his sexual attitudes they could effectively control him. But a return to a humanely moral and religious vision of man is to leave all that motivation for power and control behind; it is to give up the old myths, to challenge the new ones, and to move toward a more mature moment in human history. My contention is that compassionate religious leaders could do more for the integration of human sexuality than an army of scientists, but that they have to give up their instincts to control man in order to achieve this. I hope that any religious leaders who may read this book will understand that, although the religious observations are purposely few, it is a book written to challenge them as much as to criticize the modern mythmakers. Man needs someone to believe in and understand him, to assist him in putting himself together according to a faith and a set of values that match his nature. I think religious leaders could do an admirable job of this, but only if they commit themselves to freeing man rather than worrying about whether and what he may do wrong.

This book is also addressed to good people who are confused by the world which advertises sexual freedom so blatantly and who have come to wonder whether there are any values that will bear their weight any more. These men and women are anxious to do the right thing with their lives, not out of compulsiveness, but out of a drive toward growth. They are understandably bewildered in the present atmosphere and need both reassurance and encouragement that they are not strange and anachronistic human beings. They need to understand that not everything that is represented as a sexual break-through is actually that in reality. Many of the modern myths merely make it possible for some persons to act out their most primitive and regressive sexual impulses under the guise of being liberated at last. Still others have stayed at a very early level of development from which they view sex as a leisure-time pleasure to which they are entitled at any time or in almost any circumstances. But the primitive and the immature are hardly reliable guides to healthy sexual behavior. It is about time that somebody said so before we are overwhelmed by the myth that life is just one long skin flick in which we had better take a role or lose all chance for contentment.

This book is just a beginning but it is my hope that it will make the new myths more obvious for what they are: retreads of old and enslaving dreams. I trust that it will help to support healthy people to have more faith in their own sensible intuitions about life and love. And I pray that it will awaken some more churchmen to realize that human growth, including sexual development, is a truly religious experience that demands a constant and constructive alliance between them and struggling human beings.

EUGENE C. KENNEDY
F.S.

1
THE DYING AND THE RISING OF THE MYTHS

The pantheon of myth has had an integrated population of true and false gods all through history. Rollo May calls mythology "that treasure house of the revelations of man's self-interpretation of his inner experience and his world down through the ages." (*Love and Will,* New York, W. W. Norton & Company, Inc., 1969.) Myths let man talk to himself about what he has learned or what he thinks he has learned about himself and his universe. A myth need not be true to retain its power to control behavior and to influence personality development; the Teutonic master-race myth inspired a discouraged but muscular generation of German youth to make a good stab at conquering the world. This myth, a variation on the perennial notion of the elite or the saved, has reappeared many times in history. Myths enable men to maintain their equilibrium, to enhance their own ideas of themselves, and to keep the world in focus without having to ask too many probing and self-disordering questions.

Myths have always been associated with the primitive religious sense. Although this subject is fairly complex, it is obvious that anyone who wants to move mankind must learn how to talk to it in myths. Freud himself once said, "The instincts are my mythology." Franklin Roosevelt generated hope in a depressed people with the mythic notion of a "New Deal" just as Kennedy did a generation later with his "New Frontier." Myths energize man even as they propose to instruct him. They have flourished in the American culture, which has experienced religious fundamentalism as a continuing influence. Strikingly enough, religion and sexuality have always been interrelated in the language of myth. As important and enduring aspects of personality, they overlap in questions of human learning and meaning and they both employ ritual and generate distinctive mystiques to influence and control behavior.

Myths come and go, some falling out of fashion after science or research has battered them shapeless and, therefore, useless. Man meets a perilous moment when he abandons a myth; he must put his world together anew and this is a frightening if maturing process. So in this century, within the field of religion itself, the massive readjustment to the scholarly research on the Scriptures has popularly been termed "demythologization." This process has demonstrated that many of the literal accounts of the Bible are written in mythical language; the working out of this development has changed markedly man's ideas about his faith, its relationship to dogma, and the expectations it makes on his life. This has called for massive self-reorganization in all the churches that base their teachings on the Gospels. The laying aside of myths is paid for in anguish and uncertainty; a newly revealed truth may be compelling but at the same time painful to accept. One understands the Eskimos' saying about their own mythology and their unwillingness to alter it: "We tell our stories in the same way so that we can live undisturbed." That may be possible at the top of the world but it is impossible in the city of man. It is in that city, with all the attendant cultural and social changes that have been going on, that man has been challenged to sort out not only his religious but his political, historical, and sexual myths as well.

Some men, like the Eskimos, prefer to hold on to their myths rather than to undergo the adjustment necessary to integrate new truths into their understanding of themselves and the world in which they live. Old wives' tales, rumors, and superstitions, as noted earlier, die slowly and reluctantly if they die at all. Their stability, in the eyes of many, makes up for their distortions; they are a comfort in a world already grown dizzy through the experience of future shock. One of the reasons for the traditional dislike of prophets is that they tamper with people's myths. They dare to say out loud what persons are afraid is really true. It is not surprising that they are banished, misinterpreted, and denied recognition until a later and less passionate generation can stay its emotions to understand what they say. A prophet in any field enters its holy of holies and tears aside the curtain of myth before people are prepared to see what lies behind it.

Even though myths wear out or can be disproved, men are consistently open to new-model myths. There is a somewhat uninspected side of personality that man commits willingly to the stars, black magic, witchcraft, or the domination of a powerful personality. This side of man, permanently vulnerable because of his long-ago learned fears about sex, is pacified by myths even when they are tyrannical or misleading. The wheel of myth revolves on the underside of man as it will until he grows fully mature; man spins it to rid himself of certain notions, breathing a little easier to have them out of sight. But the revolving wheel turns up new colors and numbers, new myths against whose curve he rests his fears once more. This is exactly the process that has taken place in questions of human sexuality over the past several years. The changes in our scientific understanding of sexuality have been enormous. The prophets of this new understanding have spoken with clear if qualified voices but they have been systematically misunderstood and their findings have been systematically misapplied. Man the mythmaker is ever ready to modify new truths to conform to old fears and superstitions; what is new can be fitted out in the trappings of ancient fears; it seems easier to believe a new version of what has been proven inaccurate than willingly to embrace a changed understanding of the world.

The scientist proclaims that certain myths about sexuality can now be safely retired and, from the very truths he speaks, man fashions a new and potent mythology in which to invest himself. Several articles in the past year have listed sexual myths which are no longer acceptable in the light of scientific investigation. A new magazine, *Sexual Behavior,* in its very first issue, saw fit to read a service over a number of sexual myths which it believed had finally died. *Playboy,* with the help of sex researchers Masters and Johnson, had done a similar article only a few months before.

The dead sexual myths are many, but, as in other mythologies, the hint of future myths is coiled in the grave-side good-byes to the old ones. For example, the notion that the young man has an insurmountable advantage over the older one in sexual relations has been retired by the most recent findings of Masters and Johnson. Not only can men continue to perform sexually long after they are senior citizens, but their experience and their refined control and sensible pacing may allow them to enjoy a sex life richer than that of younger men. While this is reassuring to many older persons, it intimidates others, who for reasons very different from suspicions of physiological atrophy, find what Dr. Reuben genially calls "September Sex" a tyrannical new model against which they must measure themselves.

One of the all-time myths now reported dead is the notion that alcohol is a sexual stimulant. Medical evidence shows, of course, that alcohol acts as a depressant on the central nervous system. Drinking, it is asserted, may lead to decreased effectiveness or failure in sexual performance. But alcohol releases inhibitions and, therefore, it will not be quickly separated from sexual experience because it seems to erase the anxiety or sense of self-restrictiveness that still dogs many men. There is a tangled dynamic of self-defeat involved in this, the shifting balance of plus and minus factors which mysteriously keep a myth alive from generation to generation.

One of the great all-time myths which research has presumably put finally to rest centers on the size of a man's penis. The old ideas that a large one is important to a woman's sexual gratification and that the possessor of such an organ is more potent than a man with a smaller one have been shattered by careful investigations. This myth, however, runs deep in the consciousness of the race; to bring it up even to bury it is to make some men wonder again if science is as understanding of the implements of competent male imagery as the common man is. This myth will not be so easily interred even though it should be. Not the least of the reasons for this is the attitude of men with what they consider to be king-sized sexual organs. It will take a long time to overcome male self-consciousness about sexual equipment.

Myths about the genital organs of both men and women, despite medical evidence and available anatomical charts, have persisted throughout history. There is, for example, the old rumor that Oriental women have genitalia different in shape from those of Occidentals. World travelers, sailors, and other assorted he-men still put each other on about this supposed feature of the mysterious East. Related to this kind of nonsense is the long-time belief, paralyzing in itself, that women are to be passive in sexual relations, that man is here the master, the one responsible for sexual success. Women have, in increasing numbers, overcome this stereotype and have begun to take the initiative in sexual relations in a way thought unnatural and improbable in the previous mythic sexual commandments. The problem attendant to the demise of the passive-woman myth is that unless the man is helped to understand his role in the changing sexual relationship he fears the loss of his aggressive birthright and he dons the defensive armor of exaggerated male chauvinism.

Laid quietly to rest is the notion that not much can be done to assist those persons suffering from psychological sexual inadequacy. Nobody is quite sure how widespread this myth was, but the extensive successful therapeutic work of Masters and Johnson has proved that a great deal can be done to assist couples whose marriage suffers from some sexual dysfunction. The genuine hope that comes from this research is quickly translated into popularized notions, in the great *Reader's Digest* "Raise Your Child's I.Q." and "How to Avoid a Heart Attack" fashion. These constitute a special subdivision of the old patent-medicine myth, the promise of cures that never quite come off according to the dream of them. Too many of the moribund myths carry, like strange carrion, hatchable eggs in their thrashing carcasses.

One could add to these a list of still lively myths from the abundant folklore and rumor which are either too interesting or too convenient for too many people to set them aside completely. There is, for example, the handy myth that genital sexual expression is necessary to prevent insanity, a crazed second-cousin rumor to the old absolute of sexual wisdom that masturbation is the inevitable ruin of persons physically and psychologically. The supposed supersexuality of Negroes is another long-time favorite myth. Although their myths are overdue for interment many people still believe them with a childlike and accepting faith. These myths enjoy life after death and they have, by their supposed dying, only made room for a second generation of sexual myths, just as potent and controlling as their ancestors. Some of them have grown strong, like hospital staph, in the very environment of scientific advance that was meant to eradicate them.

Now that alcohol has been sidelined as an aphrodisiac, drugs are believed to enhance sexual functioning. However, most potent drugs, heroin, for example, obliterate sexual experience, substituting a dim nirvana for any intense sexual feelings. The self-help in sex myth is big in the age of "How to Do It" books. People who have sexual problems can cure themselves if they listen to the advice of the new sexual philosophers or if they get enough intellectual information from marriage manuals and other literature. But information, no matter how graphic, has never been enough for man. Information does not respond to the emotional components which are at the root of most sexual difficulties; by itself, information may, in fact, only cause more frustration in the lives of people who find that intellectual solutions just do not seem enough to solve their complicated problems.

There is also a new variation on the old theme of how a man proves that he is masculine. How does he now do it? Why, through being able to generate an orgasm in his beloved and, if at all possible, to deliver this simultaneously with his own. The simultaneous orgasm has become the new seal of approval on successful heterosexual relationships; it is both driving men frantic and wearing them out throughout the land. There are many variations to this notion just as there are many questions about the female experience of orgasm. The goddess of myth must have been on fertility pills because she has given birth to multiple myths concerning orgasm. There is, also, a series of myths connected with the varieties of sexual experience, some of them asserting that bisexuality is the zenith of the new coolness and the true expression of the developed personality. According to this myth, homosexuality or heterosexuality are essentially copouts from the polymorphous possibilities of mankind. Another variant reassures us that there is no way to tell the difference between homosexuals and heterosexuals and that homosexuals are more a deprived minority group than persons suffering from a psychological disability. It is also very chic at the present time for certain sophisticated women, public figures of substantial means, most of them, to sing the praises of carrying and raising children outside the legalities of marriage. This is considered a social break-through, at least on the part of the women who advocate it.

Yet another set of myths, growing rapidly in the eroticized environment of American culture, would intimidate persons who find themselves for any period of time free of sexual thoughts, longings, or plans for their next affair. This is simply not the style for the "Sensuous Man" and the "Sensuous Woman" who are presumably with it when they are self-consciously sexual and always ready for action. Not far removed are the notions that sexuality is just another physical need of man which, like eating, must be taken care of regularly. Since it provides so much pleasure, the myth tells us, only the demented would cling to outmoded ideas of self-control or the possibility of postponing or sacrificing sexual expression in view of other needs or higher ideals. This is an old idea, of course, but it is dressed now in the latest twentieth-century "sex as leisure time activity" philosophy.

Premarital sex, the narrow band of activity that has been given most attention during the current sexual revolution, is presented as both desirable, acceptable, and ordinarily beneficial for those who experience it. One must admit that this one-sided evaluation of the situation is convenient for those who might wish to engage in the activity. Belief in this myth also makes a further indictment of anyone who would comment favorably about such outmoded notions as chastity or fidelity in human relationships.

We have also come to see the other side of the coin on the issue of pornography. If the old myth said that it was always harmful, the new one says that it is almost therapeutic and that its public availability will cure all of us of our prurient curiosity about it. This does not deal with grotesque "hard-core pornography" and its possible effects on persons just learning about sexuality. Perhaps the most popular corollary of this myth is that open available pornography will cause the hugely profitable pornographic history to self-destruct.

Then there are the curious notions about sex education that make it such a hot political issue in many localities. It is almost like a screen on which people can project their own sexual anxieties and fears. Although it is not salvation in itself, neither is sex education a Communist conspiracy, or a plot to overturn the good morals of the country.

Perhaps the subtlest myth of the present time is that which says we are truly a sophisticated and sexually liberated people who have at last walked away from the religious and ethnic scruples about sexuality and into the brightly lit and comfortable fields of sexual freedomland. The core error in this myth is that man's basic problem, his failure to integrate sex into the context of his personality and human relationships—the fact, in other words, that he is plagued by sex without personal meaning and personal referents—cannot be cured by additional amounts of non-integrated and depersonalized sex, no matter how ecstatically its phrases are sung or its therapeutic effects asserted. There may be some situations in life in which one can apply the idea that you fight fire with fire, or in the language of the man suffering a hangover, to take as a cure an additional dose of the liquor that has made him ill. It does not work that way with sexuality. It is not helped by more sexuality that has been stripped of its interpersonal settings and its profound human values. This myth is inflated when it is made the only concern, or even the most important of many concerns, in a person's life. This many-layered myth, however, is large enough to bear the weight of all the other new distortions. The myth that genital sex equals human sexuality is probably the father of all the myths of the age. Both this and the multiple myths which it tends to support must be inspected more carefully.

2
SEXUAL FASCISM

Men are always fascinated by things they do not quite understand; it is hardly a secret that they are fascinated by their sexuality and that they do not quite understand it. Now, in an announcement as intriguing and as quaint as an invitation to an ante-bellum plantation ball, a sexual revolution is being held and men and women can come as they are; it is a celebration after a long night of darkness and oppression. The human race is on the verge of sexual liberation, if, indeed, it is not already enjoying it. All the villains have been punished: The censors, the clergymen, and the educators, still grim with their pitchforked *American Gothic* righteousness, have been shuffled off into exile. These withheld the light, or at least that is what it says on the engraved manifesto of the sexual revolution. Now, in the hands of hygienic scientists, we are on our way toward a bright and glistening environment in which man can give himself over to the heady dreams of his adolescence and enjoy his sexuality on a full-time basis, if he wishes, at last. A strange and hesitant aura, not unlike that which brooded over the partied *Gone With the Wind* South, hangs over this revolution as well.

The sexual revolution may be a phenomenon defined more by the news media than by other judgments of reality. What gets enshrined in our various storehouses of ephemera—such as *Time* covers or the *Reader's Digest*

table of contents—is frequently the stuff of dreams, the
things man wants to believe to be true at least for the
moment rather than the truth about the human condition.
Sex sells everything, including magazines and newspapers,
and these latter are written by men and women who are
at least as fascinated and confused about sexuality as the
average American. The panoramic and colorful documentation of our preoccupation with sex does not prove that
America has actually experienced a total transformation
in its sexual attitudes and behavior. To presume that the
revolution is complete and successful is only to compound
the sexual confusion that has hung like a mist along the
edges of the world since the beginning of time. A closer
look may reveal that the sexual revolution is not very
revolutionary and that its reported occurrence tells more
about man in general than about man as a sexual being.

Beneath all the pictures and the prose, which at least
make this the best-reported sexual revolution in history,
one still senses man struggling to understand what is going
on. Man still seems incomplete, although he continues to
make a game effort to look good; he has loosened up,
perhaps, but he seems far from liberated either in understanding or in integrating his sexuality. If anything, man
seems alone and confused; all his new information about
sex cannot lift the shawl of loneliness from his shoulders.
Even Masters and Johnson, whose feeling for human sexuality goes far deeper than that attributed to them in the
caricatures the revolution has given them as mere laboratory experimenters, recently commented on man's continuing uncertainty about his sexuality. Addressing the National Broadcast Editorial Conference, they noted that:

> The younger generation is having the same sexual
> problems in spite of sexual freedom. They're still caught
> culturally. We're at the stage where we're reading ma-
> terial but not with any objectivity. . . . With all the
> freedom to discuss the subject of sex, we still don't find
> that much increase in knowledge. We are still a society

that lives by illusions. (Reported in the New York *Times*, June 21, 1971, p. 21.)

Liberated man does not seem to understand sex very well but, for some reason, he persists in holding on to vague ideas about the way it works or should work. His two most plaguing questions, the ones he finally asks in the reassuring privacy of the doctor's consulting room, come to these: "Am I normal in my sexual orientation and outlook?" and "Can I perform adequately in sexual relations?" These are sometimes phrased by women as "Can I really let myself go in sexual relationships?" The underlying anxiety, the clawing uncertainty straining to break through the surface of the self, is pervasive. These inquiries, which have a way of unnerving the listening doctors as well, hardly come from successful revolutionaries; they are the timid and easy questions of persons who are still subject to a disturbing array of expectations and pressures about their sexual lives.

The greatest sex-education program in the United States is probably taking place in the so-called "adult" bookstores, which have found their way even into those symbols of enduring virtue, small Midwestern cities and towns where the people vote for Nixon and believe in law and order. Times Square may have the publicity but it hardly has the monopoly on this phenomenon. In pornography, as in the statistics on people and skyscrapers, New York just has more than any other place in the country. These shops, in which the intensely concentrating customers hardly ever look at each other, offer middle-age, middle-class Americans a crash course in sexuality. Columnist Pete Hamill once wrote that passing through these shops is like walking through a disease. They are filled with average people, however, not with Hell's Angels or dope addicts or other lusty-eyed fiends; they are, in fact, rather pleasant-looking Americans who seem humorless and slightly anxious as they purchase small and isolated thrills.

A proper memorial statue to the American sexual revolution would hardly be that of a muscular Greek rippling with a species of sexual self-confidence; the American sexual revolutionary would better be carved as a shivering, bony-kneed, and somewhat paunchy man whose glasses do not hide his harried look as he stands, slope-shouldered, in mismatched socks and polka-dot underwear.

We have not really passed to a new and higher plane of sexual knowledge. Americans seem ready to trade in an old set of sexual myths for this year's model. Why, one must ask, does man act this way? Something in human beings has a liking for myths, especially false ones; people resist incorporating a truly accurate understanding of reality into their general picture of the world around them. When certain faulted myths are no longer utilized, men do not necessarily trade them in for the truth. They merely transform their distortions into a new set of myths. Of no aspect of man's behavior is this more true than of sexuality. In speaking of myths I do not refer to the potent symbolic language which man employs to preserve certain truths from one generation to the other. There is, as men have long understood, a way of using the word myth as a way in which man expresses truth. I refer, however, to the misunderstandings which he willingly accepts in place of reality, the distorted perceptions according to the dimensions of which he shapes many aspects of his behaviors and beliefs.

Man interacts with the world as he perceives it. His view of reality is a product of many factors, some of which exist in the world itself while others are rooted in man's own inner needs. In any case, man reacts psychologically to the world as he sees it; for any one of us that is not necessarily identical with the world as it is. Man, however, accepts this psychological reality, even if it is marred by distortion, as the working compromise in which he lives and acts. If, for example, a man perceives the light at the intersection as green instead of red he roars through it and, if he is lucky, his perception of reality will not be tested by another driver, who has perceived reality differently, crashing into him. Man is willing to believe the worst at times, or at least the most exaggerated, scandalous, and exciting of things. These phenomena, whether true or not, reward him in ways which he has never quite understood. Men are ready and willing to perceive these things, despite mountains of contradictory evidence, or at least to entertain their strong possibility. So he reads that John Kennedy survived Dallas to linger as a vegetable in Grecian exile and a hundred other fables that make cheap tabloids profitable. There are many levels to this, of course, most of them far more subtle. The stereotype of races and religions endures and remains powerful in culture despite our efforts to purge ourselves of its effects. There is even a cyclic quality to our beliefs and practices that is almost as strong as that of style and custom. Man is still vulnerable to supersition and even this highly advanced technological era bristles with its signs, as visible as the notches men used to carve in the trees to mark their pathways through the forest. Practically no new building, for example, has a thirteenth floor; similar institutionalized superstition, second cousin to the black magic that is enjoying a second life, can be seen in many other areas of life. For a full understanding of the sexual revolution it may be more important to study social psychology than the psychology of sexuality. Man has many reasons for his psychological constructions of reality; we understand only a fraction of them.

In any case, a new crop of myths has been harvested and men, in great numbers, are giving their willing belief to them. Myth is one of man's symbolic languages which reveal something about him that we could learn in no other way. It reminds one of the techniques recently pioneered by Dr. Richard Gardner in his work with children. Children, he writes, very seldom speak to us in factual terms; they prefer to tell us stories, to use, in other words, symbols to express their unconscious wishes, desires, and fears. The trouble with adults is that we frequently respond to children factually and rationally. Children do not, in fact, find these responses particularly helpful because they do not want and cannot process rational responses to their unconscious symbolism. We literally talk a different language than they do; small wonder that communication breaks down. Gardner suggests that a person who wants to talk to children should learn to interpret their stories accurately and to respond with a story of his own containing a symbolic response that communicates much better than a reasoned reply. So it is with man and the myths in which he places confidences about his sexuality. He speaks a symbolic rather than a rational language. He lives by myths, some true and some not so true. Not all the rational information in the world suffices to answer man's questions, doubts, and fears. Rational information, which has abounded in recent years, is not enough to respond to man who communicates at a deeper and less self-conscious level. The new myths merely continue the old story of man's sexual problems and hang-ups; they tell us symbolically that the revolution has not yet been fully successful, that at a profound level man is still unliberated. Man speaks symbolically now, for example, of the intrinsic impossibility of solving the difficulties of depersonalized sex with increased dosages of depersonalized sex. He is groaning rather than uttering a revolutionary cry; he just cannot tell us why it hurts even though he knows where. Even *Playboy* and its sophisticated and smooth-talking "Advisor" column have not been able to help him. But *Playboy* at least talks a mythic and symbolic language. It is not a magazine about sex at all, although it seems so on the surface. It is rather a journal about self-confidence that responds symbolically to men's personal uncertainties. It reassures him about his image, telling him how to get it all together and where everything is at. It is a magazine of sophisticated baby talk in that its luxurious modernity quiets but does not banish man's fears.

Playboy offers a form of supportive therapy to faltering twentieth-century man, giving a quasi-effective short-term response to his chronic failures of self-confidence. *Playboy* falls in the category, a wide one indeed, of "experts" who have, with varying degrees of wisdom, been charting man's course through the mine fields of the supposed sexual revolution. Indeed, some law, deeply symbolic as well, may soon work against the sex experts, even as it has overturned experts in other fields. It is not even that some of the experts do not teach well. They are just not on to man's symbolic language, or the meaning of the myths that he hangs like a curtain across the vista of reality. Man is a problem learner because of this; he does not seem to listen, he persists in not getting it all straight, and he is still terribly afraid that he will not pass his final exam in heterosexuality.

One might note that the almost universal style of blaming the religions of the world for man's sexual problems has a mythical quality as well. Man has had a big hand in manufacturing what he wants to believe and the power the Church has had over his behavior is not something he has given to it in a completely unwilling fashion. When we are wiser we will understand that he needed the authoritarian attitudes he allowed the Church to exercise over him. Many contemporary churches have enlightened theologies on human sexuality; man tends to resist these as well, perhaps because they demand a newer and fuller maturity from him. Retreaded myths do not do this. They permit man to remain the same even though he calls things by newer names. Mythmaking may be one of the ways in which man handles change in the world around him. He shifts his labels, while he clings to his distortions at a deeper level of consciousness. Man, in fact, needs the kind of integrated view of himself and reality which only organizations like the churches can provide. When man loses an interpretative schema of life through which he can identify himself, his purpose, and his sexuality, it is difficult for him to solve the problems of sexuality because they cannot be solved in isolation from these other concerns. The principal reason for the popularity of the new generation of myths is related to the contemporary inability to see sex in the context of man and the matching failure to see man in the context of society. The intense focus on sex has excused man from a deeper and harder look at himself.

These new mythologies abound and these will be examined in the pages that lie ahead. There are two general categories for these myths. The first tells us that a new sexual dawn has come and that the world is really moving in the right direction; proponents of this myth point to the new and supposedly liberalized attitudes toward sex as their proof that this new age has arrived. The opposite myth tells us that the world is coming rapidly to an end, that the sexual revolution is a sure sign of it. The proponents of this myth use exactly the same evidence to support their conclusion. Because of the nature of myth there are many people programed to believe one or the other. We have two different interpretations of the same events and both of them are believed ardently by different groups of persons. These interpretations are, however, built more on the inner needs of the interpreters than on the true nature of the events themselves. Interestingly enough, these interpretations mark two of the great themes of man's myths throughout history, the exciting vision of a sexual paradise in which all restraints are cut away on the one hand, and the picture of a fiery new world of judgment and proper punishment for sexual excess on the other.

Sex has always made for good apocalyptic literature, especially if it includes a flaming denouement in the scenario. Hollywood, with its marvelous feeling for sex-laced biblical stories, has long known this and it has programed films to capitalize on man's fantasies in this regard. This illustrates one of man's perennial ambivalences, his longing for orgies controlled by acceptable circumstances such as their position within a story of the Scriptures, and his uneasiness if such behavior is not found out and violently judged in the last reel. This is man's way of having the best of two worlds, of letting himself experience some of his primitive longings while he holds them in check with his need to atone for his guilt at having thought of such things in the first place. It is a strange human balance that is thus maintained, the very ambiguity of attitudes which makes man susceptible to the various mythologies that surround his own sexuality. He wants to enjoy it and, if need be, be punished for enjoying it. That is easier than truly understanding it.

We cannot stop at the surface events of the sexual revolution or its varied interpretations no matter how cleverly these are keyed to man's subconscious desires. We must look more deeply into man and his partiality for myths. Even scientists are known for resisting the modification of their own myths; they do not easily shift procedures, such as testing or psychotherapy techniques, even when research evidence suggests that old tactics are outmoded or, presumably, ineffective. Oddly enough, however, men seem to get results with very divergent approaches, perhaps because of an underlying human quality which resides at levels beneath the seemingly different schools of psychological and psychiatric theory. It is well known, however, that there is a lag in psychology and other sciences between research on therapy or testing and the date at which these findings are eventually translated into practice in the expert's office. Here we have, as in the sexual revolution, two powerful myths at a standoff with each other, the one of research proclaiming that it has discovered what is actually true, and the one of practice saying that it knows what works. Scientists have even discovered the subtle role of their own expectations in shaping the results of their experimentation. Psychological studies have demonstrated that the presumably controlled attitudes of the experimenter can shape the outcome of the most carefully designed experiment. Here again the resulting data may reflect the man who collects them as much as the reality that is under study. These strange dynamics of science, as human as anything we know, have affected the interpretation and understanding of sexual research.

There is, as many experiments in social psychology have demonstrated, a certain level of suggestibility in all men that is sensitive to group pressures and opinions. This certainly operates on man's sexual attitudes, which have always been susceptible to social influences. Indeed, most individuals' explicit sex education is born in rumor and nourished on the equivalent of lurid tales from outer space;

there is little wonder that men, still more in darkness than in light, are readily influenced in this regard. They are eager believers and they look for saviors whether these are their physicians or clergymen (who may be as confused as they are), the underground press, the marriage manuals, or the latest sexual savant. In some ways, supposedly sophisticated modern man is as prepared to hand his freedom over to others and to be manipulated by those who sound like they know what they are doing, as were the Greeks who handed over their destinies to the stars. This style of sexual politics affects both men and women. This does not represent sexual democracy but a kind of sexual fascism which keeps men from their fullest development and, therefore, from their fullest human possibilities. It also prevents them from attaining sexual self-understanding. Free love is free in name only. It does not seem to make for free men any more than medieval sexual restraints did. If man is not assisted to see himself in deeper perspective than the current sexual mythologies allow, this will not be the first revolution which ushered in an era of large-scale control and manipulation of human beings in the name of freeing them. Sexual fascism diminishes man's freedom and responsibility; it therefore diminishes his humanity.

It is little wonder that man hesitates as he closes in on the next century. The experts predict sexual customs and institutions totally different from those of today; man, hardly caught up on his sexual past and uneasy with his present, is not very well prepared to face such a confusing and demanding future. So he looks back to the thirties and forties when he did not yet quite believe Freud and he had not even heard of Kinsey; he looks back at the myth of his contentment at that time and riffles through the nostalgia that reminds him of it. He hesitates and in memory wanders through these long-gone decades as a person might walk once more through the house that had known his growing up before he sets out for a country of no return.

Man the ready believer, man the manipulable, needs an

expansion of true choices about himself and his sexuality
rather than a new set of fascistic imperatives to dominate
him. A true sexual revolution will occur when man heals
the wounds in his own sense of identity and emerges with
a keener and more certain grasp on the significance of his
sexuality in the context of his own personality.

The sexual myths, however, must first be sifted and
man's eagerness to believe must be tempered by wisdom
and common sense or he will only stumble from one set
of disillusioning promises to another. Man must be helped
to put distance between himself and his myths so that he
can evaluate them with greater human responsibility
and thus with greater integrity. Otherwise his vulnerability
to the new sexual fascism will only widen. The new sexual
fascism may have swapped its austere preacher's trappings
for trailing psychedelia but it still makes the same threats
and promises to beleaguered human beings. It promises
the beginning or the end of the world but delivers neither
as it binds man with the soft and silken cord of a new
sexual mythology.

3
THE MYTH THAT SEX WAS
JUST DISCOVERED

The "new world coming" myth tells us that sexuality in an unexpurgated and uncensored form, like a lush island rising out of pure blue waters, was first sighted and claimed as free territory by the current prethirty-year-old generation. This is indeed a romantic vision, a triumph of consciousness III, but just as we have learned that the New World had regular visitors long before Columbus, so sexuality, although a land still somewhat untamed and unexplored, has been on man's maps all through history. Only a person who is a stranger to man's works and the records he has left in his caves, scrolls, and illuminated manuscripts could imagine that something new has been discovered by the counter-culture. The story of mankind teems with sexuality, and despite the recurrent use of words like "new" and "revolutionary," man long ago learned the basic facts of life about increasing and multiplying. Man has always been a searcher about sex and he has always known that it says something deep about him; he is no less different today.

It may be a shock to some young people but the new myth of trail-blazing sexuality does not hold up under close inspection. There is very little, if anything, that is absolutely new, and according to some careful analysts, far less substantial change in people's sexual attitudes and behavior has occurred in recent years than they now choose

to believe. The notion that the previous ages were inhabited by the sexually ignorant or the passionless cannot
be supported by even a casual inspection of our history,
literature, and other folkways. Sex has been threaded
through civilization and the arts as it is throughout the
fabric of human personality. Even the earliest cave paint-
ings do not depict man as an ax-swinging animal, a sexual
predator dragging women by the hair into his den. Instead,
primitive man now emerges, according to recent revisionist
comments of anthropologists, as not so primitive after all.
Indeed, it seems that he preferred to make love instead of
war and his caves are layered with appreciative depictions of the feminine form; he seems to have been more
a lover than a primitive aggressor. This is substantiated
by the discovery of the corpse of the sixty-thousand-year-
old Neanderthal man a few years ago. He had been laid
to rest on a bier of fresh spring flowers, testimony to the
fact that he was no stranger to gentleness or passion and
that those who loved him buried him with touching symbols of their regard. The feeling of men and women for
each other sings still of its enduring strength in these re-
minders of what we used to call prehistory. Today primitive man seems more a brother than a stranger.

Both Greek and Hebrew literature abound with sexual
themes. They reflect the attitudes and behavior of people
who lived long before the current sexual revolution began
to celebrate bisexuality. The Greek literature, however,
celebrated homosexuality while the Hebrew literature
emphasized heterosexuality. There is little about either
sexual orientation that has not been explored and expressed
deeply and frankly in the writings of earlier times and repeated regularly ever since. Those who feel like pioneers
in affirming homosexuality as a high, almost artful, form
of life under the contemporary banners "Gay Is Good"
have forgotten the history of Sparta, the city in which
homosexuality was a legislated part of ordinary life. They
have forgotten the lines of the lyric poet Pindar, "But I,
for the goddess's sake, waste away like wax of holy bees
under the heat of the sun when I look at the young

blooming limbs of boys." (Quoted by Frank Kingdon in the article "Literature and Sex," *The Encyclopedia of Sexual Behavior,* New York, Hawthorn Books, Inc., 1961, p. 631.) And Sappho spoke centuries ago what many Lesbians feel they have only discovered today when, addressing a young bride, rather than a young groom, she wrote, "My heart beats, my voice fails, fire runs beneath the skin, the eyes see not, the ears buzz, sweat flows off me, trembling seizes me, and, fading like withered grass, I am as one dead."

Hebrew literature offers hymns to the relationship of man and woman in a way never surpassed. Indeed, the relationship of man and woman, the whole symbolization of sexual love, is frequently employed in the Bible, to describe the relationship between God and man. This richly sexual mentality, edged always with the awareness of Israel's possible infidelity in this relationship, carried over into the writings of the New Testament and the symbolization of the relationship between Jesus and the Church. Perhaps no piece of literature has ever been so profoundly sexual as the Song of Songs. In it the lover finds his world in his beloved. She is his vineyard whose breasts are as walls with towers, whose eyes are like doves, while her hair is like a flock of goats and her teeth like washed ewes; her lips are like scalloped thread, her temple is like pomegranates, her neck like the tower of David, the curves of her thighs like links of a chain, and her belly like a heap of wheat set among lilies. The lover embraces his beloved and thinks of taking hold of the branches of a tree as he discovers in her breasts clusters of the vine and in her breath the odor of apples. Perhaps nothing has been so frank, so sexual, and so healthy in the history of heterosexual love poetry. Indeed, according to the judgment of Kingdon (p. 633), English literature treated sexuality quite frankly until almost the beginning of the eighteenth century. Sex never did go far below the surface of even subsequent writings; once the strangle hold of Victorianism was broken, a restoration of the formerly quite open attitude toward sex took place. These are only a few samples of the vibrant presence of sex throughout the history of literature—all having been expressed long before the 1970s.

For centuries, in other words, there have been ups and downs concerning society's willingness to accept and discuss sex openly. But, quietly or not, people always manage to get the hang of the idea without much difficulty. Sex has never been much of a secret; no occult combinations or mystic knowledge have ever been required. There is something in the old-fashioned idea that people just go ahead and do certain things that come natural to them. Some elementary comments and questions should be addressed to the generation which feels that it has broken the last taboos. Can they imagine, if they leaf through their family albums and look at those pious faces in their Mathew Brady poses, that their ancestors were strangers to love and passion? How do they imagine we all got here anyway? What do they think made the Forsytes into a saga? An inspection of history and its pulse in the literature and the arts reveals the current theme of sexuality and man's fascination with it. He has indeed shifted myths over the years. Who is to say he did any worse or that he was more confused or superstitious when he thought that his sexuality was guided by distant gods than he does and is now as he tries to appease the new and more demanding deities of successful sexual performance? Many will say yes, but we were ignorant then of so many things that we have recently learned. There is no denying new knowledge, of course, but it is clear that we are still ignorant in many ways and that we are only slowly unraveling the complications of sex in human life. The fact is that man has, despite his partial knowledge, always had the resourcefulness to respond to his instincts, to make sex work for him, to make it entertain and amaze him all through history. Even the tasteless and frankly erotic contemporary "sex education" movies pride themselves on tapping the ancient secrets of far-off Eastern lands and so-called primitive peoples to provide twentieth-century thrills.

The belief that sex—real sex, that is, sex without hang-ups—was recently discovered is hardly borne out by a survey of American culture. Today the hang-ups, and the young are not entirely free of them, are displayed more prominently than in any age since public buildings were decorated with phallic symbols. All people, at every age level, would be less intimidated if they realized that the secret of sex has been out for a long time. Succeeding generations have their own problems and pains with sex, not so much because of sex itself but because individuals have difficulties with the human relationships which give meaning to healthy sex life. Our civilization would be better off if we could rid ourselves of the minor conceit which claims that finally we know everything we have ever wanted to know about sex, when actually we are still working at it.

A younger generation will say that at this time people finally act on their convictions and that they have changed their life styles in order to live out what they truly believe about human sexuality. There is little, however, in the present-day passion for honesty, commune living, or group marriages that does not have a precedent even within the boundaries of American social history. The Utopians of New Harmony, Indiana, for example, fought for a freer sex morality, more reasonable laws about marriage and divorce, and also for birth control long before the present age of supposed sexual liberation dawned. According to Sydney Ditzion, "almost every social reform movement in American History carried a sexual component." (*The Encyclopedia of Sexual Behavior*, p. 86.) Commune living, heralded as a break-through in the present, is indeed a return to the past, both in the nature of the life, the customs of those who practice it, and the fundamental appeal it has made to world-weary people. The combination has always included the fusing of a humanitarian or religious ideal with a philosophy or theology of sex—and the practical reduction of these to everyday life in a communitarian setting which provided economic benefits for all participants. Thus John Humphrey Noyes invented something he called "complex marriage" at his famous community in

Oneida, New York. All the men were to think of themselves as potential husbands of all the women, and the
children were to be a source of satisfaction and pleasure
for the adults. There was even a committee on marriage
pro tem which would pass on separation when and if this
were desired by any of the members.

Advocates of sexual expression calibrated to the rhythms
of natural food diets and Mother Earth's slow turnings
would find echoes of their present enthusiasms in the number of health and diet reformers who spoke up for their
theories while the West was still unwon. Those who are
intrigued by the sensual promise of today's water beds
might remember the hydrotherapists of the previous century who regularly prescribed cold wet sheets, baths,
douches, and marriage reform. Those who delight in
public figures agonizing about their sexual convictions
need to be reminded that Henry James, Sr., using the pen
name Victor Hennequin, wrote a tract called "Love in the
Phalanstery," a plan for harmonizing sexual relations according to scientific laws. He contended that society recognized sex only in marriage and therefore it forced many
unwilling persons into a relationship they really did not
want to enter. Science, he felt, should be employed to work
out freer relationships. Those who feel that we have only
recently come to "tell it like it is" have forgotten the
famous anarchist publication *The Word*, on whose mast-
head ran a string of ideals, "free land, free labor and free
love." And they have probably never heard of Dr. Marx E.
Lazarus and his *Love Versus Marriage*, published in 1852
as his documented contention that marriage as an institution did not really support a true union of man and
woman. He dedicated it, in tones that sound currently
revolutionary, "to all true lovers, the modest and grave of
either sex."

Those who think that the era of encounter groups has
provided the first environment to encourage total honesty
about an individual's own behavior might be surprised to
read the proceedings of the "social freedom" convention

held in 1875, during which Lois Waisbrooker called for a new "standard of nature and science" that would be different from the then-acknowledged standard of authority. "To this end," she declared, "personal experiences are in order; every person must not only be permitted but induced to come forward and give his or her personal experiences; and in this free inquiry those who are as chaste as ice should have no precedence over those whose fires are irrepressible." Persons who currently think of Boston only in terms of prudery and censorship might be surprised to know that the Sexual Science Association met in that supposedly puritan city in 1876.

Aside from such historical echoes of present presumably courageous stands one must also inspect the available data to see whether they do in fact document a sexual revolution of the proportions reported in the media. One of the few careful examinations of the available data has been made by Professors John H. Gagnon and William Simon, a pair of sociologists who formerly worked at the Institute for Sex Research in Bloomington, Indiana. Surveying the available research materials on the changes in sexual attitudes and behavior in the United States (paper presented at the National Conference of the American Social Health Association, printed in *VD—The Challenge to Man*), they conclude that the changes have not been quite as substantial as men have been led to believe. Their observations support the notion that the sexual revolution has a mythic character which, if unsubstantiated, still has powerful effects on the way people interpret the world around them and on the way they conduct their own lives. That is the hidden power of myth: People believe and act as if things have changed even when they have not. Simon and Gagnon suggest three sources for the systematic self-delusion that has led large numbers of reasonably well-informed persons to believe that things have changed more radically than the evidence suggests. The sociologists identify these factors, which must be accounted as potent functional aspects of mythmaking, as:

a. A relatively recent capacity of persons to engage in public talk about sex. Until the Kinsey report, in effect, said things in public, individuals confined most of their reflections about their own sexual behavior and that of others to their own thoughts or very private conversations.

b. The way individuals talk about sex in their private worlds, like the way they talk about many other things, has a mythic quality to it. People manufacture and assent to myths because this is a way of holding their world together. This is a strong example of the way people react to the world as they perceive it rather than as it actually is. This in no way lessens the effect of the myth on the actions of individuals.

c. The conflicting ideas already alluded to in the first chapter, which variously interpret sexual behaviors as heralding a new order of things or the final Pompeiilike destruction of mankind, accentuate the impression of extremely radical change.

Simon and Gagnon point out that there is a very uneven interest in sexuality, that most people focus on the issue of premarital sex when they think or speak about the sexual revolution, and that weightier issues, such as the complex problem of what constitutes genuine masculinity, get comparatively little attention. They themselves relate the problem of masculinity to the more general social context of the difficulties experienced by individuals when there is a dilution of meaning in their work life and an evaporation of traditional opportunities to prove manhood through accepted manly challenges of hunting and so forth. They see this problem in a wider social context. They also note the lack of interest in the role that masturbation plays during adolescence in the development of the male's sense of identity and the role that its absence plays in the development of a feminine sense of identity. The discussion turns instead to the young or to the deviant which, as they note, "itself might be a substitutive form of sexual behavior." In addition to premarital sexual relationships, they cite interest in three other subjects: orgasm on the part of the female, extramarital intercourse, and the variant experience of homosexuality.

To validate the conclusion that a revolution in sexual behavior is taking place Simon and Gagnon say that the following would have to be established as true of presently young people:

1. Premarital coitus is occurring with a greater prevalence; that is, more young people are doing it.

2. Premarital coitus is occurring with greater frequency; that is, they are doing it more often.

3. Premarital coitus is occurring more promiscuously; that is, they are doing it with more different people.

4. Premarital coitus is occurring under conditions of lowered affect . . . with people they do not love.

In reviewing these conditions, the researchers conclude that it does not appear that any body of research evidence leads to the belief that the figures cited by Kinsey and others about premarital sex experience for the period 1925 through 1945 have radically changed. They believe that the data gathered by Vance Packard and presented in his book *The Sexual Wilderness* suggest that "there may be an increase in the proportion of college-going females who are not virgins," but "the ultimate meaning of these figures, however, still is in doubt." As they view them, Packard's data do suggest that for the college educated the arena of premarital coitus has moved from the post-college to the college years. There is no evidence, as they analyze the findings, however, that among those who are engaged in premarital coitus it is occurring with any greater frequency than previously. Indeed, none of the suppositions offered as the conditions which would define a sexual revolution seem to be borne out by the data that are available. Instead, Simon and Gagnon contend "logically speaking . . . that there are more conservative patterns of premarital coitus among males now than there was in the past." In other words, these analysts suggest that the measured changes in sexual attitudes are not in a more radical but a more conservative direction, that, in fact, middle-class patterns "of social life and courting have penetrated the rest of society. . . . The middle-class pattern is one of restraint and deference of gratification, and with increasing numbers of young people entering college from all social levels, the constraints of the middle class may actually be becoming more generally applied."

As to premarital sexual intercourse, they observe that this is generally disapproved but that the measures of disapproval diminish the closer this activity is to the actual state of marriage. In other words, when premarital sexual relationships are part of a larger pattern of permanent relationship in marriage, there is a greater willingness on the part of society to understand and, in some sense at least, to accept this behavior because it tends to support rather than subvert the institution of marriage itself.

The real change, as these observers describe it, occurred near the early part of the century and its effects have continued through the last fifty years. These changes were associated with larger sociocultural changes related to the First World War and the shift of the United States from an agrarian to an industrial country. Through the last fifty years there has been, in the words of these sociologists, a "gradual release of the female from the earlier constraints on premarital coitus and mate selection . . . exchanging increasing levels of sexual intimacy on the part of the female or increasing the emotional commitment on the part of the male. The romantic ideology is still endemic, as is the image of sexuality as an experience which ought to be accompanied by overwhelming passion . . . continued intertwining of sexuality and emotion before marriage seems inevitable." The changes that have occurred, in other words, have tended to stabilize rather than revolutionize the patterns of American society.

In order to prove big changes Simon and Gagnon contend that evidence would have to be offered to show that coitus among females now occurs with larger numbers of males outside the context of marital preparation and that contraception is now deemed the responsibility of the female. They also feel that "the revolution would occur when the context of values and meanings attached to acts changes, not when there are small scale differences in rates or incidences." They contend that the sexual revolution has actually been a working out of patterns of change that occurred more than two generations ago but whose effects are only now being registered on the measuring scales which have largely been applied to society only in the intervening years. In fact, the examination of the sexual practices of man in society, that is as a collective entity, is relatively recent, as is the general willingness of people to speak about sexuality in other than guarded tones and in private places. These analysts also make an interesting observation about those who look on our contemporary attitudes toward sexuality as signs of a new world coming or an old one about to collapse. They suggest that both these groups have a common delusion, "that sexuality is a primary moving force in human experience and, if it were only regulated either by suppression on one hand or by total freedom on the other, the problems that face mankind would be resolved . . . they misjudge the role of sexuality; it is by its very nature a dependent variable. It is something that is more caused than causing, and only through its ties with other human experience is it given its meaning."

Implicit in these remarks, of course, is a recognition of the dynamic power of myth once it spreads itself on the land. It does not make any difference what research shows, or what you can prove from the analysis of data. If people believe they are in the midst of a sexual revolution they will try to act as if this was true. This builds up enormous pressures, many of which push people to do things which go against their instincts, their heritage, and sometimes even their common sense. Such is the power of myth, however, and although it may yield very unsatisfactory results —people wake up with an empty feeling—it is still functionally effective in the lives of many people, especially

when it influences them at a formative stage of their development. Most human beings are, however, in a constant
formative stage of development, particularly in regard to
sexuality, the mysteries and fantasies of which they keep
often so quietly to themselves. As a matter of fact, the
analysis of Simon and Gagnon has about as much effect in
counteracting the presumption of a sexual revolution as the
fact that the earth is round has had on the Flat Earth Society of England. Man must mature in some overall sense
in order to judge the validity of the myths that urge him
one way or the other; he must learn to place his trust in
those which authentically reflect the truth of his own experience. One of the most important, if unfulfilled, functions of the churches is to make judgments on the myths
by which man is led and to help him understand those
which effectively bear the weight of his humanity.

A great deal of tension arises because of the presumptive
sexual revolution, even though the sociologists who have
been cited note, "Most young people, even those who pro-
test, are busily going about the business of mate selection
that will eventuate in marriage and children . . . What
else was really expected to happen? . . . the most important message of all this is that sex is quite frankly only the
marginal kind of drive. It does not turn off and on because
it needs to express itself. It, like everything else, needs to
be learned. Sex is only realized and sexual arousal only
occurs in social situations which are designed to elicit sexual responses." This is heresy in the heavy breathing centers of the sexual revolution, this suggestion that sex is not
a blind and demanding instinct and that much of it is
learned behavior strongly conditioned by the circumstances
in which people have become acquainted with it. The
world has been prey to the big myth that sex is untamable,
blind, and at the heart of everything. When a culture willingly believes that it is hooked on myth and tends to impose
certain distortions on all its sexual interpretations and
transactions, sex becomes a kind of life currency to people
so invested in its mythology.

The sexual revolution has happened and it has not happened. It has happened because people want to believe that it has, and it has not happened because the evidence does not suggest widespread radical changes in sexual behavior. What we need is an authentic rediscovery of sex in the context of human personality. Only this will winnow the shards and snippets of fact and impression that litter the modern scene like a farmyard after a rock festival. A first step in the right direction would be the destruction of the idea that there is anything really new or surprising in the supposed sexual revolution of the day.

4
THE GREAT ORGASM HUNT

The new measure of making it sexually has sunk deeply into the consciousness of contemporary America. Hemingway's ghost still haunts the bedrooms of the New World although he is probably smiling now at the new rules for the old test which he knew so well, manhood on the line beneath the sheets. The flags of sexual prowess are not surrendered today just for basic masculine sexual performance; they go rather to those men who can produce orgasms in the woman as well as themselves, and both at the same time if possible. This is the essence of the new American sexual myth; weary-looking men and women are seeking to meet the expectations it places on them in their sexual relationships with each other.

This myth is perfect grist for the mills of obsessive-compulsive Americans who, yielding to the machine model of man, are desperately discontent if they do not perform in a uniform and perfect way in every sexual relationship. They expect themselves to achieve the measured results of a machine with the same smoothness, efficiency, and reliability. They would even like their lovemaking to be odorless too. No perfect myth for modern Americans exists; it is a triumph for the spirit of technology. Jacqueline Susann, an unlikely prophet, caught the notion in the phrase "The Love Machine." In this mythic model man can be sexually programed and impersonal productivity becomes the abiding measure of usefulness. Appropriate techniques of quality control can ensure uniform and reliable output. When something is wrong you repair the machine and not the person. This wide-ranging myth is calibrated to two characteristics of many middle Americans: their obsessional defenses that make them prey to any dogma of perfectionism and that motivates them to pledge their loyalty to the entrepreneur who promises to show them how to achieve it; secondly, it builds into the uneasiness, raised to a fine art of being anxious by Americans, which so many people experience about their own sexual identity. They do not talk about this very much but they are certainly obsessed with it. The new successful orgasm myth provides us with the perfect combination, a compulsive response to the anxiety about sex and gender that drives so many men and women to look for salvation in the latest fad or supposed scientific finding about their sexual lives.

The tragedy is that people have even more trouble than machines do when they are fed the same program to solve very different problems. A machine so treated would react in contrary fashion, betraying its glistening and impressive appearance, coughing up nonsense instead of new equations. So it is with men and women who attempt to use the latest sexual myth as a program for the personalities which they have come to regard as a species of responsive machines. Because the sexual problems of human beings are infinitely varied, one solution obviously will not fit all of them. A single solution for everybody leads to confusion and frustration for everybody. These are reactions beyond machine experience, as is the sense of failure that cuts into the hearts of persons who cannot meet the expectations that the new myths, such as that of simultaneous orgasm, impose on them.

The present cultural preoccupation with orgasm raises many issues, both about the nature of orgasm and the nature of persons who experience it. The discussion turns our attention to the varying dimensions of the man-woman relationship including their differing capacities for orgasm. Many subtle issues are related to a basic understanding of orgasm in sexual relationships, not the least of which is the deadly potential of pitting man and woman in competition for "giving" and "getting" orgasms. The model of man as a perfectible machine suggests the presence of certain anatomical levers and buttons that must be pressed when sexual productivity is desired; the master of the orgasm is the master technician, following all the manual instructions carefully. This is part of the problem rather than any solution to the difficulties generated by the new mythology of orgasm.

America is filled with knowing looks about the subject of orgasm; these expressions, creasing middle-class faces with the squint of having heard everything, read everything, and experienced everything—the look, in other words, of sophisticated and almost world-weary wisdom—mask a state of uncertainty and confusion about sex that is almost staggering in its proportions and in its effects. Nothing is more riddled with myth than our contemporary understanding of female sexuality. The feminists argue that this is because men have tried to impose their own understanding on sexual experience that is fundamentally alien to them. This argument, not without merit, is slightly crippled by the widespread differences of opinion among feminine observers on the nature of female sexual feelings. A review of sexual research indicates that there is still extensive disagreement, even among the experts, about the nature and experience of female orgasm and that this is further complicated by confusion about the diagnosis and meaning of frigidity. One sighs and wonders if science has not given us more white-coated bad advice—and frequently radically bad as, for example, when surgery is the response to a psychological difficulty—than all the crimson-sleeved churchmen in history. The scientists have harvested their own crop of shame, guilt, and uneasiness in men and women, not because of theological specters, but because of their own inexact information and, at times, because of the compulsions generated by their own theoretical dogmas. And no religion has ever exceeded psychoanalysis in dogmatism.

The first offender, and surely the most famous is Sigmund Freud, remembered still for shifting his cigar and wearily confessing that after thirty years of research one question still eluded him: "Woman, what does she want?" It is fashionable now, of course, to observe that Freud terminated his own sexual life at about the age of forty and that what he found out about Victorian-age Viennese ladies and gentlemen might not be applicable to ladies and gentlemen in other times and other places. In the current discussions of female orgasm, the focus is on what is now considered Freud's faulty distinction between the types of orgasm. It was his position that there was an important difference between the clitoral and vaginal orgasm and so it was written into the psychoanalytic body of dogma: The clitoral orgasm represents an immature, emotionally undeveloped expression of female sexuality; the vaginal orgasm, however, represents growth and expresses the sexuality of the mature woman. The adult woman must move, then, from clitoral to vaginal orgasm. There is no doubt that this view has had enormous circulation, that it has been, in other words, a potent myth. This distinction has also occasioned great concern to many women who have been unable to experience orgasm according to the psychoanalytic template, and who have thought themselves the less for it.

Dr. Alfred Kinsey, the famous sex researcher, represents the opposite view in the sexual mythology of female orgasm. On the basis of his research he denied that vaginal orgasm even existed. He based this conclusion on the relatively few nerves on the surface of the vaginal lining (ignoring the abundant sensory supply just below the surface) and assumed that the labia and clitoris were the most important focus of feminine sexual stimulation. As a result of these widely published research findings, the mythology was rewritten to push the vaginal orgasm into the shadows and to bring the clitoral orgasm into the bright light of day. Indeed, it is clear that the Kinseyan economics of orgasm have become part of the battle cry of some of the leading feminist spokesmen in our age. They have used the Kinsey findings to deflate the male presumption that he is all powerful in producing vaginal orgasm; the Women's Lib ladies have emphasized the clitoral source of orgasm as a symbol of feminine independence. This is the very dynamic over which thousands of words have been spoken and written, not the least of them by Kate Millett in *Sexual Politics* and by Norman Mailer in his agonized rejoinder, *The Prisoner of Sex*. Perhaps the mythology is summed up as well as it is anywhere in Mailer's deeply personal reflections on Kinsey's research and the resultant conclusions about the dominance of clitoral orgasm.

Those specimen women had been tested by Kinsey. One can conceive of the laboratory conditions, and the paralysis of all the senses which may have sat on the woman, lying there, vagina open, numb as a dead tooth to that inquiry beneath the probe of the investigator's sterilized eye. Still! Only 14 per cent felt a thing. What a confusion! What a blow to self-esteem for any man. "The vast majority of women who pretend vaginal orgasm are faking it to" as Ti-Grace Atkinson says, "get the job." Damn hot spot of a clitoris. What had happened to Blake's most lovely idea that "embraces are comminglings from the Head to the Feet?" (*The Prisoner of Sex,* Boston, Little, Brown and Company, 1971, p. 76.)

Closely related to the varying opinions about female orgasm are the varying attempts to define the idea of frigidity. Most of the definitions which have been offered by clinicians, among them some of the most important and prestigious names in international science have been dependent on the accuracy of one or the other interpretations of the meaning of female orgasm. This explains the almost startling difference in the estimates that have been given about the rate of feminine frigidity over the years. Some of the researchers, restricting themselves either to the reported experience of clitoral and/or vaginal orgasm, have reported rates of frigidity up to 80 per cent and, con-

sequently, have given shape to attitudes about feminine
sexuality and its expression which have rather rigidly depended on the accuracy of these figures. These high rates
have been offered by strict constructionists of the psychoanalytic school. Most of the high statistics come from
analysts who have been treating patients for problems, a
biased population on which to base generalizations about
all women. Psychiatrist Phillip Polatin, summarizing the
results of a number of questionnaires sent to women in
the general population, suggests that, however they define
orgasm:

> 60% to 70% of married women experience orgasm
> "usually or always," about 25% "some of the time," and
> 5% to 10% "rarely or never." (*Medical Aspects of Hu-
> man Sexuality*, August 1970, p. 13.)

The efforts to define and treat frigidity have depended
on the scope of orgasmic experience considered significant
by the scientists who have elected to make a diagnosis and
to select a course of treatment. It is obvious that many
women have been markedly affected by the particular orgasm myth chosen by the physician or other consultant
with whom she discusses her sexual problems. It has also
been observed that very few people talk about their sexual
problems directly and that very few physicians, for that
matter, have had much training or sophistication in understanding the psychological or physical symptoms of underlying sexual difficulties. The tides of mythology have run
high for generations and it is not surprising that many people have been lost in this swift sea of sexual opinions.

The research findings of Masters and Johnson should
have calmed the turbulent seas. It is testimony to the continuing power of long-held myths that these rather clear
findings have been misunderstood, sometimes selectively
read, and frequently misapplied to contemporary sexual
problems. Masters and Johnson have emphasized in interviews that it is essential to understand the total picture of
the individuals involved, especially the psychological side

of their personalities, rather than to focus on one aspect of their sexual problems, in order to respond sensibly to them. They estimate that almost half the marriages in the country have difficulties and that the sexual problem hardly ever affects just one partner; sexual dysfunction is a problem of the whole marriage relationship. It is important to review what they have had to say about the questions of frigidity and female orgasm. Masters and Johnson reject the very use of the term "frigidity" because of the psychological harm it has done to women to whom it has been too freely applied. They feel that:

> Maximal meaning of the word should indicate no more than a prevailing inability or subconscious refusal to respond sexually to effective stimulation. (*Human Sexual Response*, Boston, Little, Brown and Company, 1966.)

The use of such a description reduces the rates of clinically observed frigidity immediately. It also shifts the focus away from concentration on one aspect of feminine sexual reactivity. It leaves room for understanding that a woman who does not have orgasm is not necessarily lacking in sexual responsiveness. In the same way it lessens the expectation that orgasm must always be achieved as the sign and seal of feminine sexual gratification. This broadening of focus enables observers to look at the entire complex of personality factors that have an effect on human sexual experience.

By direct laboratory experimentation Masters and Johnson have shown that the sometimes acrimonious debate about the clitoral versus the vaginal orgasm falls apart when the facts are clearly perceived. Their findings mesh with the well-known observations of psychoanalyst M. F. Sherfey who came to the same conclusions on the basis of her clinical experience with women. With the simplicity of Gertrude Stein these researchers tell us that an orgasm is an orgasm; analyzing it into its component parts, like parsing a declaration of love, merely mars our understanding of it. In other words, the clitoris cannot be considered in opposition to or competition with the vagina because the clitoris participates fully in ordinary coitus even when there is no effort to stimulate it directly. It simply cannot be maintained that there is a purely clitoral orgasm or a purely vaginal one. From the physiological point of view, the recent and most complete research demonstrates that there is only one kind of orgasm, a sexual one. Neither Freud nor Kinsey wins the day; Millett and Mailer must fight again about the sources of sexual self-esteem. The wonder is, however, that these clear findings, widely available for several years, have not been absorbed more fully into our understanding of sexuality. They have instead been partially applied to emphasize the woman's right to orgasmic experience. The findings have, in other words, been used to intensify the tension between the sexes rather than to deepen our consciousness of the significance of the overall relationship of man and woman. One is reminded of the old French saying "There are no frigid women, just clumsy men." Much of the burden of feminine frigidity may, in fact, be the responsibility of insensitive male attitudes and the peculiar masculine arrogance that has arisen from the still widely held myth that he is in godlike control of sexual experience. It is true that many men, conscious only of their own needs, are not very good at sexual relationships. But their uncertainties are only intensified when they are not helped intelligently to rethink their older myths. Despite the research of Masters and Johnson, many of these myths still prevail, pitting men and women against each other in sex rather than helping them to understand their sexuality in a deeper and richer way.

Several questions connected with sexual behavior arise in the light of the research done by Masters and Johnson. The roots of discontent run deep because these findings, along with those of Sherfey and others, have hardly lessened the tension that obtains between men and women on the subject of satisfactory sex relations at this time. There is still a great deal of ignorance and fable about questions such as these: Does a woman always have an orgasm? Is an orgasm necessary for a woman to feel sexual fulfillment? Is frequency of coitus the true measure of sexual responsiveness? Are women capable of simulated orgasm? Can a man tell when a woman is simulating an orgasm or has he been fooled with great regularity throughout the ages on this vital subject? What is the nature of the multiple orgasm reported by women? Are men capable of this? What of the question of simultaneous orgasms, fostered by marriage manuals over the last generation? Is simultaneous orgasm possible and should it be as preoccupying to a generation as self-conscious about its sexuality as the present one is?

Many women do not experience orgasm in every sexual act but this does not mean that they do not feel sexually satisfied. Clearly, a woman views the experience of sexuality as an important time of human sharing rather than as a moment in which she is convenient for the old notion of releasing male's sexual tensions. Tenderness before, during, and after orgasm is a significant source of satisfaction for the woman. Sexual activity can be quite disappointing and meaningless for her when it is stripped of its surround of sensitivity. Caresses and kisses, the expression of genuine concern for her and her happiness: These are essential for sex to be an authentic human experience for her. These, of course, are precisely what are frequently lacking in hurried acts of coitus which are dominated by the old fiction that the man is the active and dominant partner and the woman is the passive and receptive individual. That is a myth that dies very hard. It is only in relatively recent years that women have begun to feel free to take the sexual initiative and to participate more actively in introducing, sustaining, and varying the nature of their married sexual experience. A woman does not, repeat, does not have to experience orgasm in order to feel satisfied sexually in a relationship that has adequate human dimensions. This is not to say that the orgasm is of no consequence to her. Indeed, she is far more capable of orgasm than any man.

Woman is capable of multiple orgasms, and according to Masters and Johnson, these are not minor preludes to some major earth-shaking event. They are rather indicative of female sexual responsivity, the reality that a woman is theoretically capable of orgasms just as long as appropriate sexual stimulation is present. In fact, the limit of her experience of orgasm is a man's capacity for participating actively in sexual relations with her. And, of course, man is limited in his capacity to sustain stimulation. There is a great deal of confusion between the sexes because of misunderstanding the nature of multiple orgasm. This is one of the areas in which men and women are indeed quite different from one another. Insensitivity to this difference can cause a great deal of marital difficulty. While a woman is capable of multiple orgasms, man is not; he is capable of repeated sexual cycles. There is an important distinction between these concepts, one that is obscured with the vague and uncertain notions that the current mythology of successful orgasm has reinforced. Some women, for example, expect that men can react just as swiftly after orgasm as they themselves can. It is a rare adult man, however, who can immediately reinitiate sexual activity after he has reached orgasm himself. Masters and Johnson have shown that there are four stages in the experience of orgasm: excitement, plateau, orgasm, and resolution. The woman is capable of continuing almost indefinitely the experience of the third stage of this sequence; this is physiologically impossible for the man. In order to perform sexually he must pass through the stage of resolution and then begin again with the first step in the sexual cycle and he must experience this in sequence if he is to experience it at all. Conflicting expectations on each other's behavior in this regard have resulted in disappointment, confusion, and anxiety about the mutual adequacy of male and female sexual performance. In fact, the confusion about the variant needs of man and woman has increased the tension that people experience when they feel that they are on the spot in each other's eyes. In this aspect of sexual experience, perhaps as in no other, man and woman experience a related anxiety, one that runs deep inside them, but one which they hardly express or discuss very much. It is one of the fears that makes them prey to myth. As described by Dr. Roy Whitman of the College of Medicine at the University of Cincinnati (*Medical Aspects of Human Sexuality,* August 1969, pp. 55–56):

A striking paradox emerges. The chief sexual anxiety of the male is performance, but he is physiologically limited. The chief sexual anxiety of the woman concerns loss of control but she is endowed with the physiological potential for multiple orgasmic response. This major discrepancy between the two sexes thus often leads to incompatibility in sexual adjustment; he feels inadequate because he cannot do enough, and she feels guilty because she can do too much.

It is obvious by now that a discussion of sexual relationships which limits itself to a part of an experience that can be understood only in its totality may needlessly upset and possibly permanently cripple a couple's sexual relationship in marriage. This unverbalized conflict leads to the supposedly frequent simulation of orgasms on the part of women. A woman does this, observers tell us, to reassure the man about his potency. In a recent seminar on the subject among a group of psychiatrists, there was disagreement about whether a man could actually identify a woman's experience of orgasm or not. The male psychiatrists suggested that in the light of the sequence of physiological activity that has been identified by Masters and Johnson an accurate answer could be made through careful observation of the systematic biological changes which occur in the woman. They also observe that this is hardly possible because of the preoccupying nature of the experience. They add, without even a hint of redeeming humor, that any effort to measure a woman's orgasmic response in this way would be harmful to the sexual relationship. If the male must use other grounds for this judgment he is not so certain. Perhaps the best summary is offered by the woman participant, Marriage Counselor Eleanor Hamilton:

Most men think that they know when their partners
have had an orgasm, but many would be surprised to
learn how incorrect they were . . . the reason for fool-
ing a mate is likely to be expressed thus "I don't want to
hurt him; he takes such pride in thinking that he is a
good lover." Or "He gets so upset if I don't that I pretend."

It is clear that on some occasions at least, women, who
are quite healthy and mature, may pretend orgasm for
the benefit of their partners. Full orgasmic response is not
the adequate measure of the mature woman; it is not necessary for her experience of satisfaction in sexual relationships although obviously full orgasm is significant for
men. Part of the difficulty over the subject of orgasm
comes from the fact that men and women read each
other's reactions on the basis of their own experience.
Reading into what the other should experience or might
experience causes great confusion and builds up destructive expectations which only cause the man and woman
to become estranged from one another. As Masters and
Johnson have observed, "Failure of communication, on
several levels, is a prime contributor to sexual dysfunction,
making a marital unit problem as opposed to an individual
problem. It is interesting that 44 per cent of those couples
referred for sexual distress had bilateral sexual problems."
(Interview, *Medical Aspects of Human Sexuality*, July
1970, p. 31.) In other words, the basic ignorance that is
nourished by myths is compounded by a failure of men
and women to discuss each other's needs and experiences
in sexual relationships. It is not good enough just to "fix
the machine" if something is wrong in the area of human
sexual experience. In nothing is man less like a machine.
The mechanistic approach, which is reinforced by the manuals that emphasize technique, only makes worse an already difficult situation.

Closely related to this is the fact that there are varying
patterns of sexual interest at different ages in men and
women. While sexual interest runs high for the male

early in life it begins gradually to wane, although it obviously does not disappear, as he moves toward midlife. It is just the opposite for many women who begin to experience full sexual pleasure only after they reach a more mature age. These varying experiences and expectations, especially when the partners do not talk about them, also lead to mutual puzzlement. Successful sexual expression cannot be considered independent of the persons who share it with each other. Their individual psychology shapes it significantly; what they make of it they must make together, drawing on an awareness of their differences as well as their similarities. This takes constant sensitivity and, consequently, constant willingness to work through problems together if the sexual relationship is to endure successfully. Otherwise, a man and woman fall out of phase with each other. They become bored or indifferent when they can no longer make the effort to understand each other. They become vulnerable to the possibility of affairs, or they turn to the supposedly sophisticated practices of wife-swapping or orgy-going. Beneath these practices one can frequently detect sexual lives which have grown unnecessarily stale and disenchanted. Beneath these symptoms, however, one discovers a man and woman who have fallen out of touch with each other because they have never really understood some of the fundamental areas in which they differ from one another.

Perhaps the most bitter fruit of the orgasm mythology is the widespread notion that a man must produce orgasm in the woman during their lovemaking and that the ideal is for a simultaneous experience. This myth, born of the general mechanization of sex and nurtured by the sometimes overromantic and underinformed marriage manuals of the last generation, has led couples to believe that they must experience sex in some nearly spectacular way every time they come together. Perhaps the old political and economic notion that revolutions occur when there is a crescendo of rising expectations and a failure to respond to them applies here. If there is any sexual revolution it may be against the notion of simultaneous orgasm which has caused expectations in lovemaking to rise so high; at the same time, this has caused disappointment and frustration to men and women who cannot always deliver as though they were lesser gods. In this myth we see intermingled some strong characteristics of twentieth-century America: the worship of mechanical aptitude, the dehumanization of sex, and the obsessive-compulsive need to perform in the approved fashion. Not only does the secret goal of simultaneous orgasm disappoint many men and women in their experience of sexuality, it also runs the risk of diminishing their regard for each other and their understanding and appreciation of sex itself. So bent are some Americans on achieving the sophisticated style of orgasm that psychiatrist Natalie Shainess has termed them "orgasm worshippers." With repression abandoned so that people are now generally angry even at the idea of restraint the cultural milieu tends to foster this worship of the orgasm itself. Shainess says:

> Thus, a new symptom, "orgasm worship" has developed because of the discrepancy between prevailing sociocultural goals or beliefs and the possibility of attaining them. This would make it "female symptom" yet it is also "male symptom" since men, especially men with certain personality or characterological problems, often demand orgasm by their partner as proof of their virility . . . to put it simply, without love, desire, and passion, the fruits of these fail to appear. ("The Danger of Orgasm Worship," *Medical Aspects of Human Sexuality,* May 1970, p. 73.)

This myth has merely shifted the setting for the testing of a man's sexuality and of his capacity to satisfy his partner. Simultaneous orgasm has become the new measure of a man as well as the sign of a woman, the crucial symbol of whether they can really make it together or not. It would be difficult to overestimate the investment of self-esteem which men and women can make in the almost heroic effort to achieve this simultaneous orgasm. Played out on the same field are many collateral questions such as the aforementioned testing of masculine virility as well as other subtler communications about the basic attitudes of the man and woman toward each other, and the clear if unverbalized exchange of barely understood hostilities. Many men and women are trapped in this because they have succumbed to the myth that orgasm is all and that they fail as humans unless they produce one that comes close to resembling a Fourth of July celebration. Dr. Wolfgang Lederer has described part of the tension surrounding the production of the female orgasm in this fashion:

> Today the female orgasm has become to a man his last reassurance of manhood, his last proof of being needed as a man, by his woman. This he must achieve at all odds—even if his woman does not know what orgasm is, or is frigid, or may respond only to masturbation— no matter; he must be able to make her reach orgasm in intercourse, or he will feel frustrated, and castrated not only in a purely sexual sense, but in the widest meaning of the term, as a man. (*The Fear of Women*, New York, Grune, 1968, p. 281.)

Obviously, no one would question the beauty and profound resonations of the experience of mutual orgasm when this occurs in a natural and unstrained manner. The myth has made it so, however, and many couples who perceive themselves as sexually liberated are actually more hung-up than ever before because of this difficulty. As Dr. Johnson, of Masters and Johnson, notes about mutual orgasm, "As a goal, that's probably the most divisive, distress-producing factor I can think of for a sexual relationship." (Interview, *Psychology Today*, July 1969.) Yet the myth has force still and, despite the clear findings of research and the efforts to educate people better in matters sexual, the romance of the explosive orgasm retains its grip on the general population.

To sum up, there is no scientific justification for analyzing the human sexual orgasm into component parts which emphasize one physiological aspect of human sexual physiology over another. These debates are evidences of other and perhaps deeper problems in the attitude of men and women toward each other. It is clear that the discussions reflect mutual feelings of oppression, intimidation, and hostility. Some women do not experience orgasm in sexual relationships but they need not experience it in order to feel satisfied in their lovemaking. This is especially true when women experience tenderness and other evidences of human regard from their male partners. Women, however, have a capacity for multiple orgasms within the same sexual experience but, here again, sexual satiation through reverberating orgasms does not necessarily produce a feeling of satisfaction. That is a much more complex product of human exchange. A man, on the other hand, does not have the capacity for multiple orgasms and must reinitiate the cycle of sexual response in order to achieve orgasm again. This is not easily done in a short time for most men. Misunderstanding about this has caused a great deal of distress and harm to many couples.

Varying patterns of sexual response at different life stages also contribute to misunderstandings between men and women especially insofar as they read their own sexual feelings and expectations into each other's psychology. The goal of a somewhat electrifying simultaneous orgasm as proof of successful heterosexual relationships is a rampant but powerful myth at the present time that has provided a new setting for the competitive expression between men and women and has also provided a vehicle for subtler messages of stress between them as well. The strength of this myth may well be related to the larger myth that sex can somehow be successfully separated from the total personality and regarded as a natural appetite or a mechanical function. The failure of the great orgasm hunt has brought sadness and self-reproach to the lives of many people, but it also illustrates the truth that the problem is dehumanized sex, poorly treated by more dehumanized sex.

In the long run, sexuality must be seen in the same light as the orgasm itself, not as a machinelike operation full of buttons and switches, but as an integrated human act which takes on its authentic meaning and power from the motivations and feelings of the persons who engage in it. The fact that the orgasm of a woman cannot be successfully subdivided like a territory of spoils in which enemies glare at each other and say "This part is mine and I will not yield to you" demonstrates the inevitable emptiness of sexuality which is torn out of its personal context. Men and women who stand battling with the weapons of their sexuality cannot lead a revolution but they can certainly bring on a disaster. This disaster is worse than anything delivered by the forces of nature because it strikes at the very heart of life and love itself. To separate sex from the personality is to participate in the literal disintegration of man, the most offensive crime of this or any other generation. Man cannot achieve deeper understanding, peace of mind, or a sense of significance through such mutually manipulative attitudes toward what D. H. Lawrence referred to as the "sensual god-mysteries in us." One need not preach very much to note that a restoration of human values and an acknowledgment of the fact that sex is meaningful only when it is an activity shared by persons who have some regard for each other is essential at the present time. Men must first acknowledge that they are caught in the grips of myths which they would like to believe in, but which merely reflect their own adolescent strivings and their capacity to be deceived even in the age of scientific explanation. The great orgasm hunt is on and it may not come to an end until the last frustrated sigh rises from the deserted bedrooms of America.

5

THE "SEX IS EVERYTHING" MYTH

Sigmund Freud left a body of dogma and a heritage of myths whose grip on the intellectual consciousness of Western man is only now beginning to loosen. Newer knowledge about human sexual behavior has enabled us to put this admittedly powerful dimension of personality into a much better perspective. Contemporary culture is, however, permeated with notions inherited from Freud and his followers which place the search for sexual gratification at the heart of every human motivation. Psychological illness has been named the bitter fruit of sexual conflict even as personality development has been interpreted by some as the fallout from the collision between the individual's massive libidinal strivings and society's multifaceted repressive retaliatory response. The story of the human race has been written in broadly sexual terms. The arts and other signs of high culture have been interpreted as the sublimated expression of basic sexual drives. Much of this pansexualism is due to a basic misinterpretation of Freud. Nettled by overzealous interpreters, Freud supposedly said that he was not a "Freudian." Nonetheless, American culture's infatuation with pop psychology has clearly emphasized sex as the dominant motive and theme of life. Our present eroticized environment merely reflects our intense and preoccupied search for the elusive golden grail of successful sex. Psychology understands more about man now and about the other more important needs and dimensions of his personality. Sex is not everything but, because of prevailing myths, the average person is still intimidated by the thought that it is.

Before reviewing some of these, one notes that a man's perspective on sex can be altered dramatically by a change in his life circumstances. Take away a man's freedom, his job, and thereby his capacity for fundamentally defining himself as an independent and responsible provider and he becomes suddenly preoccupied with needs other than sex. Sex as the fundamental driving force recedes when a man needs food for himself and his family; it is integrated into his personality in a different way and does not ride point on the herd of human characteristics as it does in so many current interpretations of man. Failure to see sex in the more general context of personality and social and political reality has distorted its meaning and also made it difficult to many people to develop an accurate view of themselves or the world in which they live. Sex is simply not the touchstone, cure, or summation of all human behavior. It cannot even be perceived with a reasonable degree of accuracy unless a much more inclusive view of man and his world is taken into account. This is the point made by author Benjamin DeMott in his essay on several recent books on the subject of sex:

. . . Each book reveals the powerful inhibition working against acceptance, even by minds thoroughly conscious of themselves, of sex as a function of a total social reality—including high culture, low culture; artists, workers, the whole consortia together. . . . The testimony on the whole suggests that an extraordinary half-conscious, culture-wide struggle against the sense of emptiness is in process. Men and women numbering perhaps in millions seeking to use sexual experience as a means of entrance to a democratized inexpressible, hunting a way up or down toward an imagined core of existence, a center at which mystery, profundity, excitement, danger, reality (as opposed to a cultural veneer) and, above all, meaning can be known, a resource promising a heightened sense of self. (*Saturday Review*, July 10, 1971, pp. 23, 24.)

Sex is so much at center stage that people look to it for their personal salvation, counting on it as the functional dynamo of their existence, and tinkering with the machine and its instructions to set it running right in their lives. The contemporary separation of sex from love is only part of its larger separation from an authentic view of reality; overlooking man's deeper needs only compounds the frustration that arises when individuals expect so much from sexuality. Other things are more important—a sense of security, for example, without which an individual can hardly stabilize himself long enough to seek out any kind of human relationships. The wisdom that is involved in the larger view of mankind presents a difficult challenge; it demands work and promises no easy redemption through an aphrodisiac culture. A culture that so emphasizes sex diminishes its members through the massive distortion of reality which its sexual self-consciousness underscores and the meager resources of meaning it provides for its affluent but humanly poor members.

No one would, of course, deny the human importance of sexuality as a significant dimension of personality and its unique potential to express man's own identity to himself and to others. Sex, however, remains a part of man, and if it is admittedly a powerful and enduring aspect of personality, this is all the more reason for having an accurate understanding of it. The worst part of the cultural scene which misrepresents sex is that it ultimately destroys its potential richness and dilutes its human significance through its insistent efforts to overexpand it. It also removes from sex the very attributes so essential to its full experience in a proper human setting: warmth, spontaneity, and the profoundly reaffirming experience of genuine intimacy. When sex is stretched thin it becomes an erotic banner rather than a human sign. It does not even seem, if the grim-faced generation so ardent in its pursuit gives us any evidence, to be much fun any more.

Perhaps the first corollary of the "sex is everything" myth is the idea that every human being, like a radar screen turning eagerly toward the impulse that stimulates it, must be sexually at the ready every moment. The myth would have us believe that no action is undertaken, no glance exchanged, no creative image set sparkling that does not lead sooner or later to a sexual liaison of one kind or another. This romanticization of the erotic destroys the meaning both of romance and of what is healthily erotic. The dreams of glory are all sexual dreams and the person who does not aspire to be either a "sensuous man" or a "sensuous woman" is somehow badly disconnected from the current impulses of his culture. To be mature has come to be equated with being sexually active and responsive in all moods and seasons. This is sexual fascism at its worst because it imposes a uniform response on everyone, irrespective of their differing ages, personalities, or current life situations. This mythical corollary is so far at variance with the truth about what most human beings are like that it is practically ludicrous. The problem is that there is a potent reinforcement for this myth because of the strength of the intimidation that is built into it. The one thing in our culture that most people do not want to admit consciously or directly is that they are somehow uninformed, confused, or perhaps beset with even a minor problem of sexual dysfunction. No problem is more widespread, but most doctors and other consultants recognize that sexual problems are communicated to them in a symbolic language frequently of somatic complaints, rather than in direct discourse. People do not want to admit a lack of sexual skill or wisdom.

Perhaps there was no more clever book title than Dr. Reuben's *Everything You Always Wanted to Know About Sex But Were Afraid to Ask*. Nothing better captures the hard-to-admit curiosity of most people than this insightful title. The average person is uneasy about asking sexual questions and is forced to act as if he really understood many aspects of his sexual life which in fact puzzle or disturb him. This sexual fascism has no compassion for the human person because it is a blind and somewhat impersonal force generated by non-sexual kinds of commercial interest and enterprise. In fact, however, there are wide variations in the sexual responsiveness of human beings. Not all of them are thinking about sex all the time, nor are they preoccupied with the idea of getting everybody they meet into the nearest bed. Sex is simply not the only thing in their lives; when it is the only thing in a person's life, then that life demands closer inspection. It is a great relief for people when they can lay down the burden of feeling that unless they are ever ready for sex there is something wrong with them. The mystic compulsion to be prepared to respond sexually most of the time has destroyed for many the possibility of an easy and sure sense of their own sexuality.

This myth has obscured the true sources of human satisfaction which are attained only by those who have a broader and deeper view of human personality than that which constantly puts sex and its expression into close-up focus. Despite all the noise and clamor, sexuality fits best into the lives of persons who love each other and who are adult enough to be able to share intimacy in a relatively unself-conscious and affectionate manner. This seems like an old-time view of man, a message from a mummy's tomb which disintegrates in the air of its announcement. It is old-fashioned to believe that sex takes on its true significance when it is expressive of a rich and loving human relationship. It is about as old-fashioned an idea as one could espouse; it is also a true one. The myths that have so distorted sex have not helped to humanize man. They have only antagonized the difficulties which men have already known in trying to understand and appreciate the meaning of sex in the context of genuine human relationships. This is sex with a human purpose, not sex as an end in itself, as a self-justifying pleasure that needs no other human reference points. This is all part of the current myth that since "sex is everything" then anything goes in experiencing or expressing it. The difficulty is that many people are confused by the erotic ethos of the age and need to be reassured that their yearning for meaning in their relationships and in their sexual lives is a sign of a fundamentally healthy impulse toward achieving a sense of personal unity. It is sex within the context of human relationships which has been emphasized by most responsible scientists; Masters and Johnson, for example, have indicated quite clearly that their laboratory experiments were only a necessary scientific prelude to discussing the more important human problems of sex, sexuality, that is, in the context of total relationships. The myth dies slowly, however, and it has persisted in the face of abundant evidence that human beings are not always in a sexually receptive mood nor are they always restless to express their sexuality in one way or another.

The current myth has also emphasized the superficial aspects of life. This draws men away from being able to explore with greater leisure the more meaningful experiences of their lives. Much is made of the surface aspects of sexual attractiveness; indeed, entire industries, not to mention advertising campaigns for non-sexual commodities, are geared to sexual dynamics. When everything becomes sexual, then that which is properly sexual is difficult to differentiate and appreciate according to its true depths. The myth that everything is sex, however, permeates our culture to an almost staggering degree. A genuine feeling for sexuality is difficult to develop when sex is so diffused in the environment. One of the complications of this, of course, is the confusion between sexiness and genuine sexuality. Much of the erotic clutter in our culture is charge with sexiness but it is very remote from participating in anything like deep sexuality. Sexiness remains very much on the surface in its distorted emphasis on selective aspects of the human person. True sexuality is a function of the total personality and is experienced and expressed only in the lives of genuinely mature people.

When a culture emphasizes sexiness, there is a massive manipulation of erotic symbols in an entrepreneurial effort to tease the last dollar out of whatever sexual amalgam can be compounded and sold to the public. To look sexy is not necessarily to be sexual but this myth has strongly reinforced sexiness while it has not deepened human sexuality. Problems of sexual identification abound in a land that is filled with people trying to initiate themselves into the skills of seductive behavior. There is more sadness than sophistication in this and probably no sin at all. It is too superficial a human experience to make the grade as, in the long range, tyranny of this myth resides in its crippling and paralyzing effects on the true human development of individuals who, for whatever reason, are affected by it. The currency of the myth tells something about our deeper needs as a people; it reflects our lack of development and our preoccupation with the short-cut roads to the dangerously shallow sexual goals. This myth has actually caused and reinforced human fears about basic problems of personal gender identity, and because of its spurious goals it has interfered with the process of achieving real identity in the lives of many people by making them think that if they look sexy they are genuinely sexual.

When people cannot stake a claim on their own identity they are crippled in their capacity to enter into the domain of intimacy with another person. The person who cannot share himself intimately—who cannot in the memorable phrase of Virginia Masters, "exchange vulnerability" with another person—can only move into deeper self-absorption, the last stage of the stillborn narcissist. Eric Erikson's famous schema of psychological development makes the achievement of identity the task of the adolescent stage of growth. Necessary to the successful completion of this stage is the integration of sexual impulses and feelings into the personality. These are a vibrant and essential source of gender identity and, therefore, of a man's or woman's ability to experience his or her own sexuality and to express their true sexuality to others. When challenges of adolescence are not met, the individual cannot fully integrate his sexual impulses into his experience of his own personal identity. The expression of adult intimacy remains an area that befuddles and stymies the under-developed person because nobody can make a forced entrance here. One must go undefended into intimacy according to the rights automatically granted by adequate internal growth. The insistent myth that sex is everything has made the achievement of successful adolescent growth more difficult for many because the superficial and distorted interpretation of sex, which they have found in the world around them, has confused rather than sharpened their appreciation of what it means to incorporate sexuality into their personalities. The myth has forced them, often prematurely, into sexual intimacy which they can neither appreciate nor explore in great depth. It is no accident that many people seem fixated or frozen at the adolescent stage of sexual development; the reason they look this way is because that is exactly where they are. It is also where they will remain as long as the myth about all-important sex shapes their understanding about themselves and their lives.

This myth has also provided a mysterious symbolic language, the language of sexual games and sexual intercourse itself, to bear the weight of many non-sexual human problems. Many non-sexual events and experiences get incorporated symbolically into contemporary sex. This is not to say that this kind of symbolism did not occur in the past. There have, of course, been eras in which this substitution has been quite pronounced and there has never been a period in history in which sex has been free of being used for basically non-sexual reasons. It is helpful, however, to review some of the reasons people use sex to express themselves about non-sexual different aspects of their lives. This helps to place sex back into perspective and also allows us to understand how human beings frequently can misuse sex and distort their experience of it because they are using it symbolically about very different issues in their lives. Sex is not always the appropriate expression for these areas of human experience, however, and, in and by itself, it is hardly ever an adequate or automatic solution for many of the problem situations to which people apply it. This may have been an extension of the old stand-by medical advice that prescribed sex relations to patch up various problems; sometimes that works but many times it does not. Only a deeper consciousness of the true significance of sex allows people to deal more straightforwardly with their other problems. These other issues, hard enough to define by themselves, are only more thoroughly confused when they get expressed sexually rather than directly. This process then tends to weight sexuality with so many significances that its own meaning is garbled in the static.

Perhaps the oldest temptation for human beings is that which equates sexual experience with love. All too often people look for sexual experience or offer sexual experience to others as a means to achieve the warmth and acceptance that can only come in a much more generalized relationship. The premature identification of sex with love frequently destroys the enjoyment of sex and makes the development of love even more difficult. Sex is sometimes the only offering that the pathetic and unloved can make to others as they try to coax some loving response out of them. As Judd Marmor, the Los Angeles psychiatrist, has noted, "A good deal of compulsive sexual promiscuity in teen-age girls exists . . . girls who fear that they are unattractive to men, or less desirable than their friends, may give themselves sexually with a relatively little coaxing to a large number of boys in an effort to achieve popularity . . . their primary motivation is not sexual release but the wish to feel loved and wanted." (*Medical Aspects of Human Sexuality*, June 1969, p. 11.) Marmor also notes the similar motivational pattern that is found in the hysterical personality. Hysterical women have traditionally been described as girlish and seductive, great players of provocative sexual games who turn out to be incapable of true sexuality when a man takes up their invitation. They are not looking for mature sex, despite the intense and persistent quality of their seductive maneuvers. Rather, they are striving for some "pre-sexual" experience, as Marmor describes it. They are little girls, using an underdeveloped capacity for sex to get the kind of attention that children want, not the kind of love of which adults are capable. Their own internal problems are merely complicated by the myth which makes it easy for them to play out their own immaturity in public.

Sex is used as a language by the lonely, by people who are looking for some kind of human response in a fundamental and consoling way. They want sex to say that, yes, somebody else is there. When sex is trumpeted as the great key to life's problems, then the lonely reach out through it in the melancholy hope that they will ward off the terrors of isolation. This kind of sexual exchange only etches loneliness more deeply into their hearts, turning the hope for love and the meaning of sex into illusion.

Anybody listening carefully understands that many people use sex as a language through which they whisper reassurance to themselves. That is its use, for example, by the man who is uneasy about his own sexual identification and who, in a climate that so emphasizes successful sexuality as a sign of masculinity, uses it to prove something to himself rather than to communicate something to another person. Women can also do this in their own way; the narcissistic quality and motivation of this use of sex, however, is the same for both man and woman. This is perhaps the most tragic translation of all the languages of sex because it leaves the man and woman fundamentally in isolation from each other with nothing at all proved anyway. There are variants of this preoccupation with successful sexual expression in different cultures but nowhere is it more clearly emphasized than in our own. This "reassuring" use of sex only underscores the human capacity to make other persons into means to achieve our own ends. This attitude is the death of any genuine reaching out to another.

Sexuality has many other faces, each revealing equally self-contained personalities for whom genuine sexual sharing remains forever a mystery. Sex may be used, for example, as a demonstration of power, as a means to enslave or manipulate other persons. There is also the parchment-thin use of sex as a skin of sophistication; so, too, sex may be used destructively to punish others—spouses, parents, or lovers. A person can even use sex to punish himself and, in what is the most highly symbolic of all these sexual languages, it can be used to defeat rather than enlarge human communication. Some people offer sexual intimacy immediately in a relationship because this obviates the need really to get to know the other person. Sexual intercourse may be used in one effort to solve many other personal problems, although the individuals who so use it are often quite unconscious of what they are really attempting. This lack of awareness of what they are doing is the additional penalty suffered by those who are victims of the myth that places sex at the center of the universe. John Racy, a psychiatrist from the University of Rochester School of Medicine, recently made this observation about the misuses of sex:

> The sexual act should be an expression of tender feelings and wishes between two adults of the opposite sex. It should leave both gratified and neither damaged. All sexual activity that creates distance between two people or that leaves one or the other in pain, shame, guilt, or resentment is a failure and a perversion—even if its anatomical and legal trappings are "normal."

This has an old-fashioned but eminently sensible ring to it. It is the kind of common sense powerful enough to free man from the myths that have oppressed him for so long.

Man simply cannot find himself only by passing through the portal of sex. An understanding of sexuality comes only to those who first find themselves; this involves them in a far more complex human process than that suggested by the simplistic notion that sex fires all the furnaces of the universe. Sex is really something but it simply is not everything; all too often when people invest themselves in the notion that sex is everything it turns out to be nothing at all. Oscar Wilde's cynical observation that Niagara Falls is only the second biggest disappointment of the honeymoon comes true for them.

The answer to this problem is not in enlarged courses in sex education. It is rather involved with deepening the entire culture's appreciation of the real values and meaning of life itself. This confusion about sexuality challenges men to seek an authentic revolution to break the paralyzing power of a culture so desperately preoccupied with sexiness and so blinded to real sexuality. Otherwise we will be left with the reality described by DeMott:

> The fact that matters is that the startling, ugly, moving evidences of frustration and emptiness in these highcult and lowcult books aren't finally trivial. They announce that the country's true need is for a politics of institutional transformation, a cultural politics, a serious and *reasoned* challenge to its whole way of life. They mock the notion of patchup programs . . . they tell us where, drunk with the best of luck and plenty, men without purpose come out. (*Saturday Review,* July 10, 1971, p. 51.)

6

THE "EQUALITY IN SEX" MYTH

One would have to be a hard-shelled and long-gone male chauvinist to deny the charges that men have mistreated women in many ways throughout history. Evidences of the double standard in a wide variety of human experiences are still readily observable. One of the most upsetting things about Women's Lib for some men is the fact that the women are so absolutely right in what they say. The area of equality demanded for women is very broad, ranging from their careers to their political activism; it also includes the nature and relationship of male and female sexuality. The contemporary battle of the sexes is not, however, exclusively sexual, although the prevailing myths have emphasized this aspect of the struggle for a more fair relationship between the sexes. The emphasis on sex is understandable, given the central role of gender in the self-identity of all of us. In the name of sexual equality, however, a new myth has arisen to erase the differences between man and woman in their sexual experience together.

The general principle of this myth says that men and women are human beings who are basically equal to each other in every way. This gets translated into the current notion that men and women are not really different at all sexually, that they are fundamentally the same in physiological and psychological response, and that the observed differences are incidental, having arisen because of their

differing learning experiences. Much weight is put on life's
early years for a different role in society in which men
and women, coded by different expectations of gender behavior by parents and other relatives, develop separate
awarenesses of their sexual roles. These arise, as the partially true myth tells us, more from society's expectations
than from the dictates of nature. The argument is familiar,
what with boys encouraged to play rough-and-tumble
games and girls encouraged to wear frilly things and to
commit themselves to the passive and deferential mode of
relationship that used to be accepted without question as
feminine. The argument proceeds by showing the mythical
quality of many of the role expectations that are made on
man and woman in society. What is the magic, except society's, that has made women into telephone operators
and men into telegraph operators? Pointing to experiments
in social psychology that seem to negate masculine and
feminine differences in certain circumstances, Women's
Lib advocates say that we have had it all wrong, and that
what seemed inherently different between men and women
is accidentally different at best.

The result of this effort to redress the balance in the
long-distorted relationship of man and woman has generated an insistence on playing equal and carefully corre-
lated roles in sexual relations. A new set of expectancies,
identical-twin myths this time, have been forged to dominate, and in many cases, to affect negatively the sexual
and marital relationships of the men and women who try
to comply with them. Here again the obsessive-compulsive
set of many Americans has moved them to adopt dutifully
this new standard of sexual relationships. Americans want
to do the right thing; they are thus vulnerable to the new
wisdom that dictates that the sexually correct thing is for
the separate sexes to do the same thing.

Some of the biggest problems in the relationships between men and women, especially in the sexual sphere,
arise precisely from their difficulty in truly appreciating
the genuine and ineradicable differences that exist between
them on a physiological and psychological level. To ac-

knowledge and respect these differences is not to advocate a new form of an old double standard. In fact, a failure to recognize what can be considered profound differences between men and woman in their sexual responsiveness and expression contributes to making the battle of the sexes a Vietnamlike war which drags on forever with mounting casualties and no winners.

Perhaps the most common complaint of married couples about each other is their lack of sensitivity and understanding of one for the other. This can include many behaviors besides the sexual, including such incidentals as the way a person brushes his teeth or snores, but it has special importance in the sexual experience of marriage. To this very day many men, especially those disadvantaged in education, automatically presume that they understand their sexual role perfectly and that they are free to act it out with their wives whenever the urge is on them. They display remarkably little sensitivity to the woman's feelings and her possibly different inclinations; they seem minimally concerned about whether the woman experiences any satisfaction in the relationship at all. The idea of female sexuality is some vague translation of what they themselves experience. It is difficult for them to imagine that a woman has a different attitude toward and reaction to sexual intercourse than they themselves possess. Hurried and sometimes crude, pressured to perform in a way that quiets their phantom worries, these men proceed as if there were no differences between the sexes. This deformed sense of equality has caused untold pain and suffering in women who, under the pressure of a cruel and outdated double standard, have felt that their role was to accept all this in order to satisfy their husbands. It is against that false perception of the equality of sexual reaction that the enthusiastic advocates of Women's Liberation have spoken out so eloquently. They do not want to be treated as objects and they would prefer tenderness and patience, the signs of love, to an active but impersonal and unrewarding sexual life.

In this same way, some women, in the grip of other

myths or because of their lack of education, have imagined that men are capable of the same kind of sexual reactions that they themselves know. It is difficult for them to imagine that the sexual cycle in man is different from their own and that it cannot be repeated by most men very readily once orgasm has been reached. Because they have a capacity for multiple orgasms within the same cycle of sexual response, some women presume that men can do the same thing, or that they have equal powers, and these women are disappointed when men fail them because they lack the physiological ability to do this. When disappointed they can only retreat, perhaps into a permanently muted sexual life or to a position in which they look for other sources of stimulation. A false expectation of equality is, in any case, almost always disastrous because it reinforces misconceptions about the sameness of sexual response in men and women. Equality between the sexes is not assured nor very well expressed in the myth that each should perform in an identical and carefully orchestrated reciprocal manner. Authentic equality depends on men and women perceiving each other as sharing the same humanity, of rightly claiming the same dignity as persons. An acknowledgment of equality on a basic human level does not demand that no differences exist between the sexes on any other level. Indeed, this would make for a very dull and undifferentiated world.

Man and woman can only be fully understood in relationship to each other, in the ordering of one to the other that rules out conscious hurt and manipulation, in the exchange that emphasizes human dignity while it recognizes differences in, among other areas, the physiological and psychological experience of sexuality. An appreciation of these differences enhances the dignity of both men and women and heightens an appreciation of sexuality as something that takes on its richest meaning in the lives of men and women who can reveal themselves to each other in a mature and evenhanded fashion.

As the Sex Information and Education Council of the United States notes in its recent book, *Sexuality and Man*

(New York, Charles Scribner's Sons, 1970, p. 32), "A common source of misunderstanding between the sexes, either in the period of courtship or in marital life, arises from the basic differences between the feminine and masculine sexual responses and resulting behavior . . . the more women can learn about the male and the more men can learn about the female, the greater the chance they can work out compatible relationships leading to successful courtship and marriage." In clear and non-mythological terms this book details the similarities and major differences in male and female sexual responses. In addition to pervasive developmental differences, the authors discuss the variations of orgasmic levels, a truth that is ignored by those who, like surfers hunting for the perfect wave, feel that sex is a failure unless the couple find the perfect orgasm together. In this same regard, there are clear differences in sexual responsiveness and interests at different ages in the lives of men and women. While men's interests peak earlier, women may not experience a like intensity of interest in sex until they are in their late twenties or thirties. Failure to appreciate the reality of differences in sexual interest at different ages causes a great deal of psychological distress in many marriages. Only a sensitivity to differences can assist a couple to adjust in a way that enhances rather than dispirits their relationship. A lack of information and understanding about age-related differences in sexual responsivity has generated enough unsung misery and conflict already; it is only complicated when a new myth insists that such differences are unimportant or do not exist at all. Related to this, according to the authors of the SIECUS book, is a "little-understood aspect of woman's sexual life, which as far as is known has no counterpart in the male . . . the phenomenon of periodic heightened sexual interest, which occurs for a certain percentage of women at regular times of the month." (p. 33.) A man must be aware of these regular variations in the responsiveness of his wife if their sexual adjustment is to be one that reflects a healthy regard for each other. Perhaps all of this is summed up in the observation that "very little actual research has been done in this area, but the general consensus is that women are much more inclined than men to be concerned with the emotional setting within which sex takes place than with the actual physical act itself. When husbands and wives are asked to list in order the aspects of marriage that are most important to them, the men tend to put very high on the list the fact that they have available for sexual intercourse a woman to whom they are emotionally attached. With women other factors, such as companionship, children, home, security, love or affection tend to be ranked higher than sexuality. This clearly illustrates a difference in attitudes." (p. 35.) The case for sexual differences between men and women is hard to deny and disastrous to ignore if one is interested in helping men and women to reach each other and to share life more fully with each other. The new myth makes people blind to the contrasts which do not diminish but rather enhance the possibilities of their total relationship to each other. In other words, differential sexual responsivity relating to aging and other circumstances must be carefully charted and appreciated rather than mindlessly obliterated.

When men and women are urged to insist on the sameness of their sexual responses, they make themselves vulnerable to a pile-up of mutual misunderstanding and eventual estrangement from each other. Many people in our culture, however, try to act out the "equality in sex" myth and the clinical pictures of the results are hardly encouraging. As noted by psychiatrist Henry Coffin Everett of Harvard in an essay on the dangers of competition in bed (*Medical Aspects of Human Sexuality*, April 1971), men and women approach each other with real fears about how adequate they will be in the expression of their sexuality. Dogged by the current myths, they tend to set up, on some level of consciousness, charts of comparison against which to measure themselves and their sexual performance. One of these charts is the elaborate one that describes the current myth about sexual functioning. When this is the "equality in sex" myth, the young couple, already worried, are wary because they believe that their sexual reactivity should run on parallel lines up to simultaneous orgasm if they are to meet the liberated standard of the day. This intensifies their competition to stay equal with each other; certain aspects of their reactions cannot, of course, be kept fully under their control, the same way, each experiencing roughly the same thing in the other. Consequently they experience frustration, discouragement, or mutually exchanged charges of hostility; these would not occur unless the equality myth drove them on. It is at this point that the sexual relationship, under the guise of being an equal exchange, becomes the background for the kind of power struggles and infantile acting out that have been discussed earlier in this book.

John Schimel has described the philosophy and effects of this myth as it is observed by the practicing clinician ("The Psychopathology of Egalitarianism in Sexual Relations," *Psychiatry*, 25:182, 1962). The increasing denial of differences between the sexes leads to an emphasis on a similarity of expectation and performance by men and women in their sexual activity. It is not unusual to find husbands and wives bravely trying to coordinate the events of their experience of intercourse together. They are afraid to be different in their reactions lest they betray the myth of equality to which they have pledged their allegiance. They check with each other, frequently imposing the male pattern on the sexual experience, and try by every means to achieve the crowning experience of simultaneous orgasm.

Timing becomes everything for the couple so committed to traveling along the same orgastic road together. They exchange signals about their separate excitement. Sometimes this is even urged by marriage counselors and other advisers who feel that a deliberate striving for this kind of simultaneity builds a desirable richness into marital experience. It becomes grotesque, however, when the male, much taken by his ability to sustain an erection, places a clock by the bedside by which he can measure in minutes and seconds his prowess and his presumed ability to satisfy. Obviously when this kind of occurrence comes into the clinical picture, there are many other dynamics at work besides a striving for equality. One recognizes the passion of anxiety that intensifies the anxiety of passion. This is made worse by the myth-inspired compulsion to stick to each other's timetable, in a strange insistence on equality in caresses and kisses, which seems to anyone who has ever genuinely loved another person the very death of affection. Schimel reports the dream of a patient caught in the equality myth. His wife and he were in bed and they were joined by their accountant who then made love to his wife. The dreamer was not surprised because it seemed appropriate to him. This symbolically catches the outcome of a relationship dominated and nearly destroyed by a false notion of equality that budgets emotions in careful double-entry sexual bookkeeping.

People caught in this myth have unrealistic expectations about the nature of their sexual relationship and what its experience will be like. They are joined in the hunt for the elusive orgasm which will enable them to transcend all their previous experience. This is a quest for life outside the human condition, because it is built on the distorted notion of absolute equality that is outside the human condition as well. Schimel describes this very well:

> Proponents of sexual equality hold that the female, as well as the male, should progress through mounting excitement and movement to a climax of ejaculation with compulsive movements—which should be, according to prescriptions I have heard, identical to a *grand mal* seizure. (p. 21.)

These people are dominated by a commercial kind of ethic rather than by the spontaneous response of generosity and tenderness that characterizes true love. They are bartering with each other, competing in a way that reflects an inevitably destructive attitude toward marriage. The worst effect of all, however, is the erosion of their own sense of being human beings in relationship to each other.

If persons are identical in every way it may be possible for them to be friends but it is very difficult for them to be true lovers. When man and woman cannot sense each other as separate and distinct persons, if they cannot give each other the freedom to be different from one another, then their sexual lives will only reflect their overall immaturity. As Schimel notes:

Equality has progressed to the point of *interchangeability of persons and of sexes,* with the resultant loss of the sense of identity. It is hard to feel "male" or "female" if there is really no difference. The denial of differences between the sexes is one factor, an important one, in the prevalence of disappointment with sex and of actual sexual pathology." (p. 24.)

Those who are subject to the general sexual myths of our time cannot but be charmed by the notion that equality in sex is an estimable ideal. This seductive myth ignores basic physiological and psychological differences between men and women and so eclipses an appreciation of what makes their relationship rich and rewarding: the contrasts and complementarity of the sexes. It is hardly old-fashioned to suggest that sex works best when an authentic man meets an authentic woman and they are able to share their identity in the intimacy that understands their equality while it acknowledges and respects their differences. Something close to understanding the vital spark of life and creation itself resides in this truth. Pain and disillusion, as well as an eventually stupefying blandness of character and personality, are the painful consequences of falling victim to the false myth of "equality in sex."

7
SOME "FREE AT LAST" MYTHS

As a result of the supposed sexual revolution, there has been a spurt in the testimonials to the exhilarating quality of unchained sex. These pronouncements ring with echoes from earlier ages in which equally noisy declarations of sexual independence were proclaimed amid appropriate cultural fireworks. The graph of civilization is marked by recurrent jagged peaks that represent each succeeding generation's new-found discovery of sexual liberation. It is necessary to examine both the claims and the claimants because of the publicity given to them, the possibility that persons unattracted by their assembly call to newer and better orgies may feel out of it when they are really experiencing healthy negative reactions, and the danger of younger persons building their values or behavior on the models provided by these cyclic visions of freedom.

Group sex and its variations, none of them very new when one reviews the history of sexuality, promises salvation every generation or so through a broadened spectrum of sexual sharing. Now it is more convenient to classify such sexual adventures with other "leisure time" activities. There is an abundant and sometimes embarrassing literature on the matter, a subculture in which it can apparently flourish, and a familiar set of rationalizations to support it as the logical breakaway from monotonous and confining one-to-one sex relationships. Part of the myth, of course, is that everyone is tired of one-to-one sex relationships and that some new pattern, organized with characteristic American compulsivity, must emerge. As a matter of fact, however, what one-to-one sex relationships do offer on the deep and solid ground of mature intimacy is exactly what most of the group-sex searchers are seeking, even when they cannot express it very clearly. Not much psychological sophistication is needed to sense the emptiness and pain beneath the shallowness of dialogues such as this, taken from *The Groupsex Tapes* (by Paul Rubenstein and Herbert Margolis, McKay, 1971):

> *Interviewer:* Okay—suppose your kids are at the age of consent, how would you feel about their swinging?
> *Michelle:* Why should we object? It's good enough for us. We're doing something as a family without shame or guilt . . . we were at a swinging party not so long ago and a girl who is twenty brought along her mother and father . . . they were willing to experiment . . . they really loosened up and got into the swing of it. From what I hear they still swing right along with their daughter.
> *Interviewer:* How do you feel about this, Tom?
> *Tom:* It was beautiful, just great, to see a mother, a father, and a daughter able to communicate with each other on such a deep level . . . how many kids can go up to their parents and tell them that they met this guy or this girl and had intercourse with them without the father or mother tearing up the place?

Indeed, group sex presents itself as the servant of the confused masses, not only freeing them from taboos but improving their general human relationships at the same time. In another dialogue in the book, a girl named Melissa is asked whether she ever experiences jealousy or competition with her mother over the same person:

> Maybe we did go to bed with the same man at this party or that, but it wasn't a planned thing. Sometimes we don't even know this happened until a couple of weeks later when we're talking about a guy who was some-

thing special. Then it may come out: "Wow, wow, I
know who you're talking about! Oh yes, that guy was
super . . ."

And the following testimony from Angelo:

Once you break a cultural taboo, you're through the
wall and you realize how artificial and unnecessary the
barrier was. You see people and ideas boxed in all
around you. Many times you're able to discover doors
and walls that are not visible to others, and answers to
questions and problems as well.

Not many experiences open life up quite so dramatically; small wonder that swinging sex has achieved such
notoriety. It is peculiar, however, to discover in the midst
of the sensual feasts described in this text, a glint of a
deeper and more painful hunger. It is a classic example
of how sex is once again being used, somewhat blindly
to be sure, in an effort to experience some sense of human
meaning and significance. A man named Scott testifies:

I feel that in certain swinging groups you can reach an
intense closeness with people, not always sensually, but a
strong bond between people can be created. I have been
surprised to find a lot of people who want this kind of
closeness, a tribal feeling of concern for one another in
sort of an extended family as opposed to one-to-one,
individual selfishness.

Group sex is part of a deeper human quest, a sign of
something missing in life that is not very well covered
over by the "free at last" brand of myth. One cannot escape the impression of loneliness and alienation and the
hollowness of failed intimacy in their own marriages in
the lives of so many who commit themselves to liberation
through group-sexual experience. The very superficiality
of the favored rationalizations tell us that something more
must be understood about the isolated and puzzled people
who are looking for a religious salvation through swinging
together.

The same quality runs through much of the documentation of the new swinging style of living. There is, for example, enthusiastic testimony from other persons who are involved in one or the other form of group-sex experiences. A young couple report that they have engaged in group sex for the last year and have also carried on one-to-one affairs outside their own marriage. The wife, a teacher at an exclusive school in New York, describes group sex as "an art form." Her husband agrees, saying, "It's life art, even though we are married, we are growing as people, and marriage should have to do with spiritual growth, not sexual exclusivity." (The New York *Times,* May 10, 1971, p. 38.) And what might provoke jealousy, the interviewer asked the husband? One quotes his answer, not to ridicule it as much as to sense the poverty and immaturity that went into its manufacture, "We do get jealous. But it's about things we are insecure about. We are secure about sex and our relationship together so we don't get jealous about that, but if a guy takes Mimi out to an expensive restaurant, I might get jealous because I can't." This is pathetic testimony to the profound need for a much truer liberation of the personalities involved in this and similar relationships.

This is typical of the smooth but superficial reasoning that various oracles provide in order to make the new myths of freedom seem reasonable and enticing. One is reminded of the bits and pieces of *Playboy* philosophy which are so carefully contrived to reassure the underconfident and anxious American male. Building on their advertising philosophy that accepts no copy that would in any way make a reader conscious of personal inadequacies (therefore no ads for finish your high school education, etc.), *Playboy* is a compendium of the slick but shallow persuasions that make a new vision of free sex seem like paradise regained. Perhaps a classic example of this superficial thinking was the response given on a David Susskind television program by a young girl who worked as a "bunny" in one of the Playboy clubs. She denied that the activities of "bunnies" amounted to a refined kind of prostitution.

The bunnies had been told by those who prepared them for their work that after the customers had a good time at the club they would go home with greater sexual interest in their wives. The bunnies were practically evangelical in their promotion of marital harmony, or so they had been helped to believe. But as one observer noted, with the kind of question that cuts through this rationalization, when the husband is then having intercourse with his wife, to whom is he making love? Does this make his wife into some substitute instrument for fantasied infidelity? These are difficult questions, however, because they make people confront themselves and the dimensions of their presumed freedom. There is frequently not much to them; their myths are as thin in substance as they themselves are.

As Benjamin DeMott notes in his review previously mentioned:

> But over and over you grasp as you read that as any of the presumed identities—as parents, say, or "heads of households"—few of the "subjects" have better than a shadowy existence. The fathers have had little father-hood: cannot discover themselves as figures of mystery in the eyes of a child studying a grownup's mastery of a craft, cannot be teachers of values or skills, cannot instruct on ethical opinion, cannot be held responsible by anyone, even themselves, for the fates of their young . . . they are diminished beings. (*Saturday Review*, July 10, 1971, p. 51.)

By their own testimony, and by the evidence of research done on them and their activities, these liberated people come across more as searchers than as discoverers, as people who, having been deceived by an old and repressive myth, have eagerly embraced a new salvation-promising version. While these phenomena have occurred frequently in history, they cannot be written off as inconsequential to the future course of events. These people are not just sociological statistics; they are men and women who are in pain, who are deprived emotionally, and who are using as an antidote for their own experience of disintegrated sex large doses of even more disintegrated sex. The myth says that they are establishing new sexual freedom; the truth tells us that they are trying to cure an old and desperate loneliness.

Radical innovation in sexual life style seems rather the symbolic expression of other life conflicts, as can be noted with the new crop of mothers, many of them well-known public figures, who are raising children without entering into marriage. Since these ladies are well known they can afford to live above and beyond the masses who cannot feel quite so free of society's traditions and institutions. Many of these ladies are actresses who make no secret of their living, at least from time to time, with men of their choosing, and of bringing their children into the world. They also state that they intend to raise the children on their own instead of in the context of what they look on as an outdated concept of "normal" family life. There is nothing rare about women raising children without husbands; the tragedy, in some ways at least, lies in the lives of those who can afford to do nothing else. Our culture is filled with people who, not through such independent choice, are left with the children of husbands who have long since deserted them. These mothers have become famous as the scourge of welfare-law reformers; some ladies of the stage and screen, on the other hand, have attained a new celebrity because they have chosen and can easily afford to live this way. What is not considered in these stylish arrangements is the long-range fate of the child. It is not inappropriate to wonder just what symbolism is involved in this defiance of convention, what tales of previous conflicts and frustrations, what stories of pain and deprivation have gone into the making of these decisions. It is fair enough to say that it is the business of these ladies and no one else's. The possible impact of their actions, well documented in the popular press, suggests that what they do in public they must also take responsibility for. In the long run, it is the child who may pay the price for growing up without a father or with only a vague idea of the man from whom, whether the child is a boy or girl, so much that is essential to full personal development must be learned. Such arrangements may be fine for the mothers, but it is entirely possible that the children of such unions will have emotional reactions to them sooner or later. It is rather well established psychologically that in ordinary circumstances the nature of the relationship of the man and woman in any family is the most powerful influence on the development of the children. When this is lacking or faulted for some reason, suitable substitutes for the missing parent may be found in available uncles or other friends of the family. Perhaps the need for a stable pattern of male-female figures is adequately handled in the relationships of celebrities who choose not to marry but to live together anyway. But it is also possible that the notoriety, uneasiness, and the possible unconscious factors that occasioned the relationship in the first place may have an ultimately telling influence on the development of the children who are born into these arrangements. The women who grant interviews about their new liberation may be telling us about an old and very personal psychological enslavement from which they are trying to work themselves free through this new life style. Here again, what they are doing is symbolic and has little to do with sex. It is not quite as free as it looks, and although it may meet the needs of the single mother, the child's needs may very well be slighted in the process.

It is interesting to note the number of young couples who establish similar relationships and who, in the ordinary course of events, even if they persistently avoid the formalities of marriage, gradually institutionalize the pattern of their living together. There is little difference between the patterns of stability that they impose on their relationships and those which they would experience in conventional marriage. They are not quite free from the kinds of things which people do spontaneously once they have begun to live together. A close examination of how they live shows them to be less than revolutionary—and not quite as free of human social processes as they would like others to believe.

Typical of the new freedom for actions that "don't hurt anybody" and that produce agreeable sensations is the widespread and mostly unqualified endorsement of masturbation. There is no doubt that masturbation has suffered from a horrendous mythology for centuries. Undeveloped religion, superstition, and man's perennial uneasiness and unwillingness to communicate fully about his sexuality have conspired over the generations to make masturbation a wicked and perverse experience, one capable of corrupting a person physically and psychologically, and of rendering him unfit for marriage or life in public at all. These destructive myths have increased man's anxiety and burdened him with a great and unnecessary sense of guilt. Superstition about masturbation still thrives in many areas with resultant hesitancy and uneasiness about this subject. A more sensible and compassionate understanding of masturbation has been achieved during the last several decades.

The churches themselves have come to re-evaluate their moral positions and to free masturbation from the absolute category of serious sin, although this does not automatically undo the suffering that human beings experienced when they were tortured by the false theological misinterpretations of this developmental experience. A new masturbation myth abounds at the present time, however, one that says man is free at last in this regard. Perhaps we should have expected this myth as the logical overreaction to the very distorted views on masturbation that were held so strongly for so many centuries. Masturbation has passed from the myth of sin to the myth of virtue. It is, in the words spoken by a genial "sex expert" on a late-night TV show, something not to worry about at all, just "the second best kind of sex." There is discernible eagerness in many presumed experts in mental health to proclaim the therapeutic quality of masturbation. It is good, they say, as a substitute for regular sexual relationships and it cannot really do people very much harm. One can almost hear in the statements and writings of some of the experts, the testimony of persons freeing themselves from the burden of their own religious tradition and anxious to tell us about it. This myth of the virtue of masturbation is a convenient way to express personal experience which, while significant for them, may have little to do with sex itself. They are telling us that their old religious code no longer enslaves them.

While it is clear that it is impossible to classify masturbation as a sin, it may not be quite so easy, nor so prudent, to glorify it in the way that has been done by many of these authorities. It is good to purge the concept of masturbation of any overtones of moral wrong but it would be unfortunate to think that it is of no psychological significance. Masturbation cannot be understood unless it is seen in the context of the overall personal development of the individual.

If we keep emotional growth in mind, we can understand that during the period of adolescence the individual must consolidate all the aspects of his growth and experience into some kind of stable identity. He does this in order to prepare himself for the next developmental step which leads him into mature heterosexual relationships. It is in the midst of this process, and with significance for the process itself, that masturbation appears in the lives of growing human beings. It is a source of sexual pleasure but it cannot be regarded merely as this or one will ignore the other dimensions of what it means in an individual's life. When masturbation occurs, it is a sign of a person dealing with a problem of his own growth. Through masturbation he experiences himself in a new way and catches a glimpse of an aspect of his identity which will have great importance in the next phase of his development. He senses himself, in other words, as a sexual being, whose destiny is to grow toward being able to share his complete identity in the general expression of sexuality and marriage. Masturbation becomes a dynamic kind of event, giving evidence of the individual's efforts to move beyond the regressive and primitive elements so characteristic of sexuality at an earlier age in his life. It is, in other words, a sign of growth, a sign that the person is indeed getting himself together in order to move forward in the life cycle. He is doing something about his identity in a profound way, accomplishing a task whose resolution is highly important for his further development.

Masturbation is not excluded from the category of sinfulness because it is so common; it is excluded rather because it is a mark of growth, a sign of a person putting himself together rather than seeking a disordered experience of sexuality. Masturbation is better understood in the whole complex process of human growth; it is part of the way in which a person deals with a transitional growing together of the sexual dimensions of his personality. Masturbation does not have any harmful physical effects on the individual, despite the lingering stories of terror which were so common when it was looked on as the action of a degenerate. It is more difficult to understand it psychologically, especially in adults who have presumably achieved their identity. One must examine the fantasy life of the person who masturbates. This gives a key to understanding the meaning of the action in the individual's life. One cannot a priori say that masturbation is a matter of indifference. All kinds of things can come vividly into the minds of human beings, especially into the minds of adolescents, so fantasy must be evaluated very carefully. When the fantasy accompanying masturbation is a regressive and infantile fantasy that recurs in regular fashion, this is ordinarily a sign of a serious growth problem that cannot be dismissed as having no significance. A person whose fantasies are of a very undeveloped kind of sexual activity, and if these recur on a compulsive fashion, is probably struggling dynamically against some deep inner block to his continued growth toward maturity. A fantasy of a person committing fellatio on himself, for example, as cited by Peter Blos in his book *On Adolescence* (New York, The Free Press, 1952), expresses the individual's defensive struggle against homosexuality. "Masturbation," Blos says, "assumes pathological features whenever it would consolidate regressive infantile fixations." You cannot shrug off this kind of problem and say that it is a matter of indifference whether the person ever resolves it or not. His freedom may be noticeably diminished by those who, without hesitation and without reservation, tend to endorse masturbation as a source of pleasure, as just another leisure-time activity.

It is also significant to note that masturbation can be quite isolating, even when there is no sign of any deeper difficulties, and that it is frequently used by the individual to combat depression. If a person grows to depend on masturbatory activities, this may also impede his development in relationship to other persons. If he finds the locus of all pleasure in himself, then he cannot pass through the further stage of being able to share himself, which is essential to his complete growth. Masturbation in marriage can have many meanings, as widely different as persistent immaturity to unconscious expressions of hostility to the spouse. It is a complex question and the myth that tells man otherwise does him a great disservice.

Perhaps the most subtly deceiving myth of the present moment flows from some of the assertions of the Women's Liberation movement. Today's women, at least through the ladies who speak for them, have insisted on breaking the grip of male domination and of asserting a rightful sense of their own individuality. Supermale, even Super-Mailer, writes in self-doubt in the face of these ladies. Women are free at last but, ungentlemanly as it may seem, the myth must be questioned: Who is getting free? The answer comes just as clearly: why, men, of course. Do not let Mailer or any of these other ruminative males fool you. Men are winning again, freeing themselves from mature obligations in fundamental and far-reaching ways. Men are, as a matter of fact, the real beneficiaries of this version of the "free at last" myth. With their complaints disguising their pleasure, in the way of men throughout history, they have allowed women to back into a new high-style bondage as the price for some of their isolated victories in the battle for Women's Liberation.

Little attention has been paid to this fact. Perhaps men like it that way—a little darkness, a lot of anonymity, and a quick drifting away from the point of responsibility that is at the heart of the man-woman relationship. Just as it happens in so much bad fiction, real-life men have slipped into the night leaving their women not so much free as abandoned, not so much liberated as alone in the face of complex problems centering on *her* sexual life. Woman has come, in other words, to have the buck stop with her, neatly placed there by a quickly vanishing and suddenly immune male figure.

It is the woman, after all, who must take the Pill; it is the woman, in this new-found freedom, who is to decide whether she will have a baby or an abortion; it is the woman who must bear the weight of rebelling against the destiny which she no longer believes to be linked to her biology. Yes, women can decide these things, but while some women boast proudly of their capacity for independent self-determination, it is legitimate to ask whether women should be deciding all these things alone. The myth makes it that way but is it, in fact, psychologically sensible or even morally permissible to let man escape so easily from such difficult problems? Is man really uninvolved or above and beyond the law? Put briefly, men have never had it so good; they can step away from the exploitation of women, they have taken care of female needs, and now they can let women make decisions about the consequences of their behavior with men. Men have not commented on this very much, probably because they know a good thing when they see it. They can continue right into their old age sowing wild oats, rationalizing their behavior with the conviction that woman alone must answer the hard questions about sexual responsibilities. The question, then, is not concerned with a woman's right to decide whether or not she will have children—although this is the only thing people seem to talk about these days. Beneath the controversy lies the profound question of what, in the long run, is to become of individuals and the human race if man is exempted from his responsibility for giving or withholding life in relationship to a woman.

This is to cheat the woman and to make her a captive

while seeming to free her. Her liberation becomes an illusion and she is left isolated with a myth that is empty of consolation. No longer the victim of constraining laws or ivy-choked Victorian customs, she is the victim of a view which has far more serious oppressive possibilities—the willingness of men to employ rationalization as a substitute for wisdom in the conduct of their relationships with women.

This gives man a great out, the escape route of his dreams, a treasure suddenly stumbled upon, the value of which is so staggering that a man dare not breathe a word about it even to his best friend. Unfortunately, such sudden wealth unworked for, such mindless excuses offered gratuitously tend to make a man irresponsible because he never even needs to think about whether he also shares some responsibility for the consequences of sexual experience. He is free now to be superstud, far freer than woman who must bear the burden of the sexual mistakes and face up to the hard decisions of whether she will bear new life or not.

This is hardly a brave new world; it is, in some ways, more timid and less assertive than the old one. The consequences of allowing man to move off into the unmeasured distance as woman deals with the questions of conception and abortion are numerous. As social observers have noted, there will be obvious effects on family life and on the role of the husband and father as the maker of any decisions at all. At a time when many American men are judged to be somewhat passive already, and where a man's capacity to define himself as a male is important for the healthy family life, his further diminution as a decision maker is bound to have consequences not yet counted. This possibility, suspected by few men at the present time, logically proceeds from allowing the woman to bear so much of the burden of whether children will be born or not. The decisions about how they are raised are already largely in the hands of women. Whether man will have much of a formative or influential role at all is a fair question. He will be paying a high price for feeling free as a sexual adventurer. Here again, however, the price may not be paid so much by the man as by his children. In the same way, one can expect further changes in the relationship between man and woman, a slow and subtle restructuring, the effects of which may not be noted for many years. There is nothing new in these observations; it is just a question of time before the predictions of contemporary social analysts show up in real life. What people have not speculated about much is whether the alteration in the man-woman relationship will, in fact, lead to a healthier and more mature exchange between them, or whether it will lead to a further fragmenting of their relationship in the future.

Perhaps the most important issue centers on the nature of the guiding values which have allowed the present situation to come to pass. It is almost epically remarkable that, despite the tumult and shouting about birth control and abortion, few, if any, churchmen have addressed themselves to the questions implicit in this version of the "free at last" myth. Few words have been spoken to stress the responsibility of the man's participation in all the sacred decisions connected with family life and the raising of children. Perhaps that is because churchmen, being males for the most part, all suffer from the same kind of narrow vision. There are many questions which must be discussed about the role of women in contemporary society but it is difficult to imagine any of them which do not also involve men. Neglecting to discuss the implications of this pseudoliberation of women perpetuates the male myth and sentences the discussion to suffocate in its own rhetoric while it leaves the fundamental question of man's responsibility untouched. The issue is too large for a TV talk show, too far-reaching to be left in the hands of highly verbal but otherwise not very well-qualified discussants. Aside from literary figures, hardly any men have seriously addressed themselves to the major issues involved in Women's Liberation. It may well be time for the churches and universities, for all those institutions which see themselves as committed to the preservation of human values, to search out the full dimensions of human liberation, both male and female. Otherwise there will be no end to the myths, only new versions of the same old enslaving deceptions.

8

THE "AS LONG AS NOBODY ELSE IS HURT" MYTH

The sexual revolution, as has been noted, has been narrowed for many to the question of whether and for what reasons premarital sex may have increased in our day. The Sex Information and Educational Council of the United States interprets the research findings on this question much as do the sociologists Simon and Gagnon. Both attribute the impression of a contemporary sexual revolution to the increase in the population and the greater public discussion of such issues as premarital sexuality. Both emphasize that the largest changes in attitude took place around the time of the First World War and that the consequences of these changes have been working themselves out ever since. What is occurring today is the logical development of the widespread societal transformation which occurred fifty years ago; it is also an outcome of our unique tradition of an open and free courtship system. Another analysis of the current data by Professor Keith Davis of the University of Colorado says that the effects of these more remote causes may be measured in the shifts in the sexual behavior of college men and women that have taken place during the last decade. Although he believes that college women are having more sexual experience earlier and probably with more partners than was true before 1960, he concludes that "As dramatic as these changes are, they hardly justify the term 'sexual revolution,' for to a considerable extent the changes are related to changes in moral standards that show considerable continuity with the past." ("Sex on Campus: Is there a Revolution?" *Medical Aspects of Human Sexuality,* January 1971, p. 142.)

Most analysts suggest that even if the changes are more revolutionary than they are prepared to admit they do not break sharply with traditional outlooks and patterns of American marriage-oriented relationships. They support this with the interpretation that intimacy occurs increasingly in the context of relationships that have a personal significance for the partners; in the phrase the somewhat cold-blooded statisticians use, "affection is present." In other words, the couple like each other and so they go to bed together. Analysts associate this affection-related behavior with a new disapproval of promiscuity and a preference for a partner who is valued, at least to some extent, as an individual for himself or herself. The Sex Information and Education Council believes that America has four premarital sexual standards:

Abstinence, the formal standard forbidding intercourse to both sexes; the double standard, the Western world's oldest standard, which allows males to have greater access to coitus than females; permissiveness with affection, a standard growing in popularity, according to which intercourse is accepted for both sexes when a stable affectionate relationship is present; and permissiveness without affection, according to which coitus is accepted for both sexes on a voluntary basis regardless of affection. This last standard has a quite small number of followers, but is most newsworthy and thereby misleads the public as to the size of its following. (*Sexuality and Man,* New York, Charles Scribner's Sons, 1970, p. 40.)

It is against the background of these findings and these interpretations that young men and women in college confront the question of their own sexual standards and practices. The atmosphere, even if it is as misleading as the experts tell us, is still charged with the expectation that the young will have to deal with sexual expression before their graduation from college. Even if some merely accomplish this in fantasy, it will still reflect basic attitudes toward themselves, other persons, and the values by which they will lead their lives. Sometimes the young find themselves adrift on what seems to be a strange and silent sea; they are expected to find their own way across it, but without reference points; this is a bewildering and frustrating task. So it is for many young people at the present time who live on a terrain shaken constantly by tremors. Even if these do not register very high on the sociological Richter scales, they still make it seem like a sexual earthquake to those caught on the trembling ridges. The myth, no matter how inexact, continues to shape attitudes and behavior.

The new morality, properly understood and appreciated, emphasizes individual responsibility in each separate situation; it is the shifting referent for many who are faced with decisions about premarital sex. The sharp focus on the individual situation pries it loose to some degree from the setting of space and time; the new morality, however, does not intend to isolate itself from previous moral traditions or from the public effects of its application. The new morality is seldom appreciated for what it actually is: an extremely demanding ideal, perhaps one of the highest moral ideas ever offered, which is effective only in terms of the maturity, self-knowledge, self-discipline, and honest judgment of those who propose to employ it. It does, however, emphasize the responsibility of the individual to inspect carefully his own circumstances and the possible consequences of the decisions before him. Insofar as the question of premarital sex is concerned, the new morality demands a careful self-search on the part of both the man and the woman, a penetrating and genuine honesty, and a willingness to see beyond the moment to the near and far reaches of their responsibility. What people forget, of course, is that although the new morality emphasizes the situation, no situation can be torn completely away from the context of the personal life histories, values, and other relationships of those involved. There is no such thing as a human situation which can be pulled free of all other moorings. This is as true of premarital sexuality as it is of any other situation in which a true human choice is involved. The new morality does not, as the caricature has it, say, "Do what you feel like." It is much tougher than that.

Myths beset both the new morality and the question of premarital sexuality. Although it comes swathed in many wordings, one of the favorites emphasizes the notion that an action is morally acceptable, in this case premarital coitus, "as long as nobody else is hurt." While this is easily asserted, it is not quite so easily measured, not for the individuals immediately involved nor for the other lives which theirs may touch and possibly affect quite deeply. The "as long as nobody else is hurt" myth is a romantic notion, one that closes the situation off from the rest of the world, chopping it away from the context of the life that precedes it, and the existence that follows it. The heightened tension and mutual self-concentration that often accompanies the moments of decision about premarital sexual experience may make a young couple feel that they are truly hidden from the rest of the world in each other's arms. It may not be entirely fair to rest the weight of this myth on their perception of the universe, however, because it is as unreal a view of life as that in the stylized fiction of movies and women's magazines.

One seems a spoilsport to raise such issues when it is high tide for romanticism, at least according to the oracles who read a lot into the box-office success of *Love Story*. Yet it must be said because the human capacity for self-deception is hard to overexaggerate. This is surely the case in the emotionally charged and intense circumstances in which a young man and woman are faced with a situation in which it is very difficult to be sure that no one else will be hurt. The first concern, of course, should be whether they hurt each other or not, and if this seems like a hard question, it is appropriate, given the analysis which tells us that premarital sexual exchange seems to be occurring more in the context of relationships marked by mutual regard and affection between the young man and woman. If this regard is present, then the question of whether they may hurt each other is more relevant now than ever. The presence of affection in the relationship makes the decision harder, not easier, when it is taken seriously. Affection is a word, after all, with many meanings and the couple should know the depth and strength of what they mean by it. This is especially important if this is the first relationship that has seemed to mean anything to the young couple, or if it is one in which they are just beginning to awaken to the mysteries of themselves as human beings. In any case, it cannot be lightly asserted that the immediate decision to have sexual relationships is devoid of the possiblility of harming anyone. Despite the presence of affection, the act itself may have long-range consequences in the lives of persons whose own personalities are just forming.

Part of the problem, of course, is that the young have been left quite on their own by some institutions to which they would normally look for help and advice. They have been cut away from the context of the rest of life but not entirely of their own will. Many adults, yearning for the youth they did not seem to have or that they fancy they lost somewhere, have made some mystical identification with the rising generation and in the process have abandoned their own responsibilities as mature guides and instructors to them. When the older generation fails to provide a reliable moral content the young will reject it or mistrust it. Something like this seems to have happened, especially in sexual matters; the young have generally concluded that many of their elders have demonstrated a certain reticent hypocrisy on this subject. Growing persons —and anyone who works with youth today on the college level realizes that they still are in the growing stage—need the supportive presence of adults who are in full possession of themselves and are, therefore, capable of helping young people to become more adult as well. Growing persons need nothing quite so much as older people with whom they can establish healthy relationships that become a passage to wisdom for themselves. The young need the active rather than bewildered assistance of educational and religious counselors who are secure in their own identity and who work through their own judgments on morality in terms of their own life experiences and their own traditions. In other words, the young need people who believe in something and who have had to work at understanding what they believe. One of the clear signs of maturity is the presence of a philosophy of life, and often there are scars to show for it. An internalized set of beliefs, by whatever name it is called, enables persons to evaluate their life decisions in terms of some clear reference points. People who possess principles are trustworthy; it is through relationships with persons who have achieved at least a relative maturity of their own that younger people are helped to internalize a stable set of ethical principles for themselves.

Mature adults do not focus only on sex all day long; they can help younger people to place sex into a rich and deep human context. This is not done by rhetoric alone. Sex is put in perspective only as we interrelate with persons who have managed to integrate their own sexuality into their personalities. In other words, to help persons make good judgments on their sexual behavior, the best course is not quick advice or cutting them loose to do what they feel is right; it is rather to help them to grow totally so that all their powers of judgment can be brought to bear on an aspect of their life which cannot be successfully isolated from the rest of their personality. When you cut people loose from their values and traditions as though these were of no consequence, when you isolate them to decide about matters such as premarital sex solely in terms of their personal reactions to each other, then you have, in fact, isolated sex from personality in a new and more sophisticated way. The question involved in premarital sexual decisions frequently demands an appreciation of whether this is some preshadowing of integrated sexuality or whether it is an example of disintegrated sexuality. It can represent either; only a close look reveals which is authentic. Giving people advice that tears sex out of its human context simply does not help them answer the challenge of getting it back into context in their own lives. So for example, the father whose only concern about his son is whether he has packed his contraceptives, has not helped the young man's growth; he only thinks that he has. Part of the difficulty for the young, and for all of us for that matter, is that adults who live by well-internalized principles are hard to find. Until we do find them, we can expect that the "as long as nobody else is hurt" myth will continue, in a somewhat unexamined way, to prevail.

The myth needs careful examination for many reasons. As has been noted, many elders endorse an unrestricted kind of freedom for the young and then abandon them to make their own way through it without charts or other points of reference. Sexuality is also a prime area for the rationalization of behavior. When this is done subtly and swiftly, the smooth characteristic of all unconscious defense mechanisms, we hardly know that it is going on. The reason is because the rationalization fits into our plans so well. And the air is full of prefabricated rationalizations these days; pleasure is the new measure of what we do and everyone else is doing it; it is such good experience to have before marriage; well, the world may end tomorrow and why not? It is also important to remember that premarital sexual experience is a prime setting for the use of sex for non-sexual reasons. The sexual experience of this young man and this young woman may have nothing to do with their relationship or their sexual feelings for each other. This first experience of intercourse or this particular experience for this couple may have a symbolic meaning that can be understood only in terms of other relationships and experiences in their lives. It may be, for example, the dramatic expression of rebellion against parents, or the assertion of one's independence. Premarital sex can serve as the validating testimony of virility or of femininity for persons uncertain about these. Premarital sex can be a manipulation of power rather than a transfer of affection.

These are all possibilities; if honesty is essential to making a good decision, then these notions, unromantic though they may be, must be considered.

Sexual intimacy that is easily and quickly given may serve to short-circuit the possibilities of experiencing a truer and richer intimacy in the relationship. If persons share sex before they have truly come to understand themselves or to know each other, then it may be difficult for the relationship to develop much further. They may have a good time, in a sense, but that is not the same as growing in love for each other. Obviously this cannot be said of all cases, but it has been clinically observed that a relationship which comes quickly to the sexual level may never get beyond it; at that level, for as long as it lasts, the persons can stay strangers to one another. Giving sex easily protects them from experiencing the kind of vulnerability to hurt that is necessary for the true revelation and sharing of the self. Sex is easier to give if its gift is not an opening to but a protection against hurt; if anything breaks up the relationship, then nothing much is lost. These kinds of relationships, of course, are signs of deeper difficulties beneath the surface, signs, in other words, of people who are searching but, who in effect, are using each other whether they recognize it or not. Sexual intimacy does not, of itself, make individuals more mature. Not all the myths in the world give the sex act in itself the power to make persons grow up. Its premature presence in a relationship can, in fact, be a sign that the individuals have not grown up. It is hard to be sure that no one else will be hurt unless people ask themselves about their deepest motivations and attitudes toward each other.

Obviously, some young people approach each other through a developing affection and knowledge that are the prelude to a genuine kind of intimacy. This, however, should be able to stand the test of close examination and bear up with the trials of delay and separation that are so much a part of ordinary life. Young men and women can truly become friends and grow very close to each other in a loving and responsible way. It is to validate this healthy, growing relationship that the presence of mature adults is needed, neither as opponents nor enthusiasts for the young couple, but as reliable persons with whom they can discuss their concerns and their ideals. These adults, incidentally, will not use the phony arguments that have never worked very well in terms of helping people to make responsible decisions about premarital sexual intercourse. To stir up fears, to use threats, or to guarantee that they will not enjoy it; these are arguments that are ridiculous and will only contribute to the untrustworthy image of the older generation. People who use these blunt instruments really kill more than they give life; they also convince the young that they do not understand them and that they are really out of it.

Neither, however, should the pseudoliberated cast aside religious traditions or other cultural inheritances as though these were of no consequence for the couple who judge them important in their lives. It is currently popular, and apparently fun for some, to ridicule or to toss aside completely an earlier religiously oriented education. Bad or old-fashioned religion is an easy target, as is most every other system in the human condition, for that matter. It is a dangerous business, however, to try to uproot a person from his beginnings and the culture which shaped him. Those who indulge in it may contribute to a sense of alienation, premature and ill-understood; no man can cut away his roots without knowing just what he is doing. The individual who does examine his own beginnings and sift through his own educational experience in the light of his present situation, the person who is, in other words, trying to think out his own moral position, deserves admiration and encouragement for doing what is properly human —pondering the important experiences in his life and trying to integrate them with his present knowledge and the decisions he now faces. The individual who takes these judgments seriously and tries to review them in the context of his life experience is truly developing himself. He deepens himself as a person and thereby ensures that whatever decision he makes will be a measured and fully considered one.

There are things to be said in favor of persons who choose not to engage in premarital sexual experience, although these are not said out loud much any more. We live at a time when the arguments in the other direction seem to predominate but there are many, including some distinguished psychiatric authorities, who argue against the "as long as nobody else is hurt" myth. Thus David Mace, in a recent symposium on premarital sex, summed up his position this way:

> Sexual behavior surely is an expression of personality patterns. It has been established in all the major studies of marital adjustment that girls and boys who have been virgins before marriage make better adjustments in marriage and are less likely to divorce than those who have had premarital sex relations. This is a consistent finding. Virgins are better marriage material. The question is why. The answer appears to be simply that these individuals don't indulge in premarital sex relations because they are people with ego-strength and with conventional attitudes; they are the ones who do well in marriage. (*Medical Aspects of Human Sexuality*, November 1968, p. 21.)

Another psychiatrist, Dr. Beverly Mead, has supplied some supportive reasoning in defense of chastity, which might be required reading for all those who are touched by the myth that things are all right as long as nobody else is hurt. Mead notes that the residue of the double standard makes it easy for the young man to get away with premarital sex but still leaves a burden on the young woman who cannot walk so freely away from the consequences of some of these experiences. As to the question of premarital sex's value as a learning experience, Mead notes that frequently premarital sex teaches a person quite unhealthful things, especially if the relationship is disappointing or frustrating in some way or another. When sex is experienced in adverse circumstances, it may well hurt rather than deepen the relationship of the young man and woman. If the experience is a negative one, the effects of this may linger and distort or cast a shadow over the meaning of sex later on in the person's life. The woman is especially vulnerable in this situation because she tends to associate sexual experience with love and is bitterly disappointed when the young man does not. As Mead notes, "She may feel disappointed, and in some cases may even feel cheated or used, particularly if the boy does not become more romantically inclined toward her following the experience, and so often he does not." (*Medical Aspects of Human Sexuality,* January 1970, p. 13.)

The assertion that if love is present it will solve all the problems does not hold up in the light of experience. Love is a complex and at times a contrary thing, and what feels like love may turn out not to be very lasting or substantial. The ones who are then hurt deeply are the young people who, with the best of intentions, have followed the shadow of myth more than the substance of reality. The generation that is presumed to be mature owes more to the growing generation than to leave it on its own, equipped only with a vague "situation ethics" and an urgency to carry on "as long as nobody else is hurt." If that philosophy comes to prevail, then we can be sure of one thing: All kinds of people will be hurt.

9
THE "THIS WON'T HURT YOU A BIT" MYTH

People used to claim that pornography was corrupting and dementing and it could lead to criminal acts. People don't believe that any more. They have discovered that it was a myth built on overstatement and so they have turned to a new version that is the mirror image of the threatening old tale. Now it is fashionable to say that pornography cannot hurt you at all, and that it may, in fact, be good for some people at some times. The most fashionable indictment, to be leveled with the sigh of a man who has seen it all, is that it is boring. This is part of a larger mind set with which the pseudoliberal of the age surveys the world around him. It is a species of the faith whose main creed is that censorship must be opposed at all costs and in all circumstances. A lesser tenet of this faith holds that obscenity cannot be defined legally; therefore, nothing definite can be decided or said about it. The orthodox line says that absolute freedom must be accorded to the publishers and vendors of pornographic material on the theory that the more it is available the less people will want to purchase it. Denmark is the model country in this myth, where, the legend tells us, the repeal of the obscenity laws has caused no rise in the rate of sex crimes. Many claim that Danish sexual freedom has been a success, but it is still too early to solve American problems with another country's incomplete experiments. First of all, we must try to understand the American experience where, indeed, a large measure of freedom already exists.

This myth is built on a strangely absolute orthodox faith, that there can be no interference of any kind in the regulation of pornographic materials, a strange absolute indeed in a land that delights in celebrating the relative character of most situations. The new morality hardly has room for absolutes, but there is nothing relative in the insistence that pornography is good dirty fun and that it can hurt no one. This same somewhat curious outlook opposes violence in every form except the pictorial, the verbal, or in some other electronic or graphic form. "It is a part of life," the true believer says, "and we live in a violent world. We should see it as it is."

Many liberals are so intimidated by this absolute myth that they doubt their own common sense at times and hesitate to make the kinds of sensible decisions that place pornography into a better perspective of judgment. One hardly needs to espouse puritanism to realize that pornography has become a major problem exactly in proportion to the greater freedom that has been granted to it in the United States. The fact that a lawyer or a judge finds it difficult to define what is obscene does not mean that a man of common sense cannot tell the difference between what is healthy and unhealthy, between what is decent and indecent in the description and pictorial representation of human experience. It may also be dangerous to assert that pornography is totally harmless. This is especially true for some of the materials which depict primitive and pathological sexual practices. All these issues, since they are strains of the same mythic web, deserve discussion.

First of all, the decreasing controls over pornographic materials have done anything but lessen their availability or their commercial appeal. The underground sex which was supposed to wither away in the atmosphere of complete freedom has flourished instead. The underground has, in fact, moved out of the slimy cellars and above ground, turning certain sections of great cities into scabby collages of high-rent sex shops. These have not only flourished, as, for example, in midtown Manhattan, but they have burst their former fairly well-defined boundaries and spilled over into other parts of the nation's great cities. In fact, there is hardly an American town of any size that does not have an "adult" bookstore with its shaded windows and redeemable fifty-cent admission charge to capitalize on the erotic interests of its patrons. In a front-page story, the New York *Times* reported the results of a survey conducted by that newspaper on sex exploitation in midtown Manhattan. The following were the reported highlights of the survey:

A. Organized crime now dominates most of the pornography business, and there is strong evidence, according to Police Commissioner Patrick V. Murphy, that it has considerable control of prostitution through the pimps.

B. Business men and their associations are fearful that the sleazy, sometimes frightening atmosphere created by prostitution and pornography is a serious threat to the world famous theatrical district and the restaurants and hotels that depend heavily on it.

C. There are strong indications that Supreme Court decisions liberating interpretations of obscenity and pornography were instrumental in persuading organized crime to invade New York and vastly expand the porno-sex business.

D. Constitutional lawyers discern rising public indignation that may make the city a forerunner in a national backlash movement . . . even while the porno-sex business grows, some operators profess to be upset that profits are no longer as great as before, claiming that this is the result of overexpansion. (The New York *Times,* July 11, 1971, p. 1.)

The New York *Times,* surely one of the most distinguished and liberal newspapers in the world, has thus presented strong public charges that legally available pornography does not self-destruct but rather proliferates like a strange cancer that begets allied diseases in the wake of its own explosive growth. The catalyst for all this, of course, is organized crime whose sure eye for commercial profit has never been proven keener than in the present situation. The *Times* has editorially urged the New York City administration to do something about the sex-shop inferno of midtown Manhattan. This newspaper can hardly be classified as in favor of censorship, having defeated the government over this very issue in connection with the Pentagon papers only a short time before it published its survey of sex exploitation.

There is no doubt that it is difficult for lawyers and judges to define pornography and obscenity in a manner that allows for intelligent legal or judicial proceedings. It is a big jump, however, from acknowledging this problem to concluding that nothing is obscene and that anything and everything are allowed in the home, in the mails, or on the counter at the corner drugstore. The myth tells you that it is all in your mind, just as beauty is all in the eye of the beholder, and that we are paralyzed in any effort to define for ourselves or for others the essence of pornographic materials. It is, however, dangerous to think that because you cannot define something legally it is impossible to judge it as immature or inappropriate to human dignity.

Perhaps the claim that obscenity should be legalized because there is no rise in sex crimes in places where this has happened is the strangest argument of all. Common sense tells us that this is a minimal requirement when wise men make a decision or write something into law. That there would be no increase in sex crimes seems the least one could expect from any worthwhile human proposal. The question that must be asked is: What other changes occur, what else happens to individuals or to society, what kind of learning or conditioning takes place, and how does it affect individual growth and cultural development? These are more difficult questions and they are harder to measure but they refer the issue to the situation in which we must make a judgment on it. Are there effects from

the products of the porno-sex enterprises which are negative for human beings, even if they fall short of making
them demented or leading them into lives of sexual
criminality?

Common sense is a great help in saving oneself from
the convolutions of the "this won't hurt you a bit" myth.
Common sense, after all, refers to the sense of the community of intelligent and mature persons who try not to
kid themselves about life and its meaning. To the assertion
that nobody can tell what is dirty or demeaning any more,
common sense says, "Like hell you can't!" The problem
of the lawyers and the judges is not the problem of the
common man trying to lead a decent life, pay his bills, and
raise his children with a chance for happiness. A reasonably healthy person can tell you what is obscene and
he can do it without raising his voice or even blushing with
embarrassment. Mature people have a reliable set of reactions to what is right or wrong, healthy or sick, conducive
to growth or destructive of it. They do not rely on statistics
on sex crimes as their guide to judgments about books,
photographs, or motion pictures. They know that sex
crimes are an extreme index of behavior and that what is
important is whether certain materials and their use really
build and reflect human maturity. Well-developed personalities simply do not require nor seek out exotic erotica for
isolated thrills; healthy people are hooked into life in a substantial manner that enables them to make quite accurate
decisions about the shoddy immaturity of the pornographer
as artist and philosopher.

Common sense tells us, for example, that organized
crime is not concerned much with aesthetics or anything
about the common man but his dollar bills. Pornography
is not boring to the criminal and the fact that lawless
elements have taken over and expanded the pornographic
enterprise in America is hardly a comforting piece of information. There are few signs that the people who buy
pornographic materials are finding them any more boring
than they ever did. Pornography has been a growth industry whose only problem, like that of many more respecta-

ble businesses, has come from overexpansion. Common sense tells us that skin flicks, massage parlors, live sex shows, and other erotic materials are more than "boring." They are also immature, self-centering, and frequently quite primitive. Assorted erotica do not represent nor help others to see man in his full potential nor do they assist human beings to understand love and sexuality as healthy aspects of the mature personality.

The myth tells us that pornography cannot hurt us but no less a group than the presidential Commission on Obscenity and Pornography discovered in some of the research that is not frequently referred to that certain aspects of pornography can be harmful, especially to persons who are in the formative stages of life. In other words, certain depictions of bizarre and perverse sexual practices may go counter to healthy psychosexual development. It is to the lurid and exhibitionistic variations on sadomasochistic themes to which the attention of concerned adults should be turned. The achievement of fully developed sexuality is a complex process and it can be affected by certain kinds of stimulation and certain capitalizations on primitive erotic impulses in the individual. The bewildering array of available erotic materials that are built on sadomasochistic themes indicates one of the sexual hang-ups with which America has not yet adequately dealt; it also illustrates the dangerous distortions to which the growing person is especially vulnerable. Medical evidence and intuitive wisdom tell us that this kind of exploitation of regressive sexual themes is not quite as harmless as people might like us to think. There are consequences to conditioning a person to certain forms of sexual excitation, especially to themes which degrade and dehumanize the person and the meaning of his sexuality. There is nothing new in this, nothing surprising for that matter, except for the fact that the myth holds that all this is at least neutral if not good for us. It is difficult to write off so easily and almost cheerfully the powerful effect of regressive erotic stimulation on the developing human being. It goes against the objective of growth which is to integrate sexuality in the context of loving relationships with others. Primitive and distorted erotic stimulation does nothing of the kind. It does provide thrills and orgastic experience by fanning the sparks of the elemental and base-metal residue of human personality. Kinky sex is not a triumph but testimony that the sexual revolution has not freed men from their hang-ups; it has only allowed them to act out their wildest fantasies in the movies they make and the books they sell. This is a form of violence against the audience, a species of rape in which the rapist grows rich as he cheaply ravishes the curious.

It is important to note that full maturity is a state that relatively few human beings have reached. While we may like to think that we are completely developed, the fact is that most of us are unfinished as human beings. There is not much public admission of this, although there are many unobtrusive signs of it, not the least of these being America's fascination with pornography. The major implication of the fact that most human beings have not achieved their full growth is that many adults are still at a formative stage of life, much in the way their adolescent children are. In other words, when we reflect on the possibly damaging effects of erotic conditioning on growing people, we must refer this possibility to a far wider population than that of children and teen-agers. An adult is not defined automatically by his age; he reveals himself in a number of more demanding measures of maturity. The American flirtation with pornography, even in its less virulent forms, explodes the myth that we are a sexually knowing and sophisticated people. It suggests that even adults who presumably can mind their own business are not immune to the psychologically damaging effects of erotic presentations which emphasize primitive and regressive themes.

Perhaps the most obvious area of kinky sex which needs restraint if not total censorship is the association of sex and violence in books and in films. This has always been a potent erotic combination and there has been an increasing emphasis on it in our entertainment. *Variety* reported in the spring of 1971 that the motion picture industry, disappointed at lowering profits for sex films and worried about the rejection of its rating system by the Catholic and Protestant film boards, would de-emphasize blatant sex and replace it with violence. This shows the cunning intuition of the businessman whose commercial heart tells him exactly what lever to press in order to capitalize on the voyeuristic longings of his audience. In the depiction of sex and violence, human beings are used as objects to provide kicks of various sorts to an audience ready to buy that kind of sexual stimulation. Sex and violence can be associated very subtly or very obviously; the effect is the same in the long run and it is hardly one that enlarges man or contributes to the integration of sexuality in a positive way.

The new myth tells us that none of this makes any difference, but the old truth about man reminds us that it really does. You either understand man as a person whose destiny is to grow to his full potential or you disfigure him by making full growth difficult or impossible for him; man's psychosexual development is not something that proceeds irrespective of the human interventions and stimulation, the quality of relationships, and the dignity with which it is perceived and treated. Man is susceptible to many influences and in no place is he more vulnerable to deflection from full growth than when he is sweet-talked into selling out his psychosexual development for a primitive mess of erotic pottage. The great freedoms that our American distrust of censorship is meant to guarantee do not include the freedom to distort and cripple the psychological development of human beings for commercial profit. This is exactly what the "this won't hurt you a bit" myth does and it is time that the common sense of the common man rejected it.

10
THE "WE ARE SURE OF OURSELVES ABOUT SEX" MYTH

The discussion of sex is intimidating for most people because man's uncertainties about himself are easily dislodged. Most persons are not, nor can they be expected to be, completely finished psychological products. They spend their lives dealing with the progressive challenges of human growth but they seem never to be complete; in no area of growth is this more true than in sexuality. The integration of sexual behavior is not a smooth or directly uphill process for any person. Society's shifting attitudes about sex, the multiplication of myths, and an individual's sometimes fluttering pulse beat of sexual reactivity: These make the average person uneasy about talking freely of his sexual feelings, fantasies, or other experiences. Indeed, the person who is given to much talk or bragging about his sexuality is an old and familiar type, the man who uses static to hide the surface noise of his own imperfect sexual adjustment.

Man likes to be reassured; that is the business of magazines like *Playboy*, which is marvelously orchestrated to build a smooth but superficial shield of self-confidence around its readers. The true genius of *Playboy* rests on its capitalization on human uncertainty rather than on sexuality itself. It makes a man feel sophisticated, not only through the relatively harmless inspection of highly retouched photos of young ladies, but also through slickly packaged advice on ordering wine, driving sports cars, and knowing the combination of tie and shirt that define one as a man of the world. It is senseless to condemn men for being lustful in reading such a magazine: They tell us rather of their willingness to settle for an antidote to their persistent uneasiness about themselves as sexual beings. *Playboy* complicates the picture for man, of course, because it so subtly prods him to live up to a highly polished ideal, the veneer of which barely covers the cracks of uncertainty in his psyche.

Man will admit to almost anything before he will admit that he has sexual problems. We have made these so difficult to talk about, so unsettling in their ultimate implications for human beings, that many people speak about their sexual problems only in symbolic ways. For example, while pretending to a reasonable level of sexual sophistication, they buy almost anything that promises them new information, assistance or reassurance about their own sex lives. The sexual revolution has seemed to take place because only in relatively recent times have people verbalized questions that have bothered them for generations. It is important to recognize this uncertainty and to deal calmly with the multileveled reality of sexual experience that is found even in the healthiest of people. Healthy persons are not immune to sexual conflict, or to a whole range of unexpected and sometimes frightening sexual fantasies and impulses. Of such is the stuff of man's sexuality made: It becomes integrated, not by oracular advice, but through the growth process which consolidates and gives increasingly mature shape to the patterns of adult sexual expression and experience. Mature sexuality, sex which fits in and is coordinated with the rest of human personality, is no easy goal to attain. "The sexual life of a human being," L. E. Sissman writes, "is a delicate balance between the ideal and the real, between the pragmatic and the impossible, worked out painfully over a period of years—adolescence and early adulthood—until an accommodation, an adjustment that will last for life, is finally arrived at." (*Atlantic*, August 1971, p. 24.) This observation, as so many others made by literary rather than by scientific people, catches a good deal of the truth about the long and frequently agonizing process by which a human being comes to terms with his sexuality. Man's sexual awareness and experiences have been subjected to so many strange modes of repression and liberation throughout history that he now stammers uneasily and unnecessarily in their recounting. The band of normality is quite wide, and we have only begun to understand the complex issues that are involved in human sexual development. One of the most cruel of the current myths makes man cower as it proclaims how sure we are of ourselves about sex.

As a matter of fact, we are not sure about many things connected with human sexuality. It is a subject dominated by theories which, like the warring churches of Christendom, give widely different explanations of observed facts. It is no wonder that man's sensitivity about his sexuality is aggravated by the bewildering array of opinions and advice, many of which claim scientific validity, that confronts him. An unending flow of periodicals and picture books adds to the clutter of sexual myths that surround modern man. A classic example is *The Sex Book* (New York, Herder and Herder, Inc., 1971), which takes a strange moral pride in its graphic pictures of sexual organs and frank textual comments. The book is, however, heavy-handed, and despite the clarity of the photographs, it generates more fog than sunlight. It is a product of superficial entrepreneurial minds rather than of genuinely searching human beings. In reviewing it for *Life* magazine (July 16, 1971), Dr. Michael Halberstram wisely notes that there is more wisdom in the autobiographical sexual philosophy of a man like Norman Mailer than in the pseudoscientific nature of *The Sex Book*. Indeed, one of the great difficulties in the explosion of information about sex is the varying depth that is evident in the attitudes and convictions of those who write about it. Norman Mailer is not fully informed scientifically about sex but he is a profound human being who, despite his own obvious problems about sex, has thought long and deeply about the meaning of human sexuality. He is, in the long run, a better communicator than many of the self-assured experts on sex who, smiling genially, hand out information that does not really inform. A serious personal search into the matters of human sexuality is infinitely more valuable than a superficially applied set of scientific conclusions.

Another difficulty involved in man's search for reliable information is the relativistic viewpoint that is characteristic of many sexual commentators. What they speak of dogmatically has few reference points by which the average person can judge the answers to the sexual questions which bother him most. These latter can be summed up, as has been noted, in the anxious worry about whether the individual is really normal or not. When normality is a totally vague concept, when anything goes, then it is almost impossible for the average person to have a clear idea of what adult sexuality might be like for him. There is a modern tendency to back away from identifying healthy elements in human sexuality and instead to leave it wide open, like an electrical field that can host an infinite combination of impulses, in a totally indifferent way. These confusions stem, I believe, from confusion about the use of the word *normal* itself and from our failure to acknowledge that we are still in the foothills rather than on the summit of the mountain of sexual understanding.

Normality can have as many meanings as a scientist wants to give to it. He can refer to normality as a statistical concept which indicates the range of responses which are characteristic of the largest chunk of the population. It can be used as a form of moral judgment which is imposed on different human actions. As a result, what is normal has been identified with what is virtuous just as what is abnormal has been identified with what is sinful. So, too, normal can be used in the favorite meaning of the commentator who employs the word: He can, for example, suggest that any behavior which leads the person to the experience of erotic pleasure falls within the range of what is normal. He can also use the word normal, as I believe it is still possible to do despite the culture-bound character of these judgments, to describe that behavior which is recognized as healthy by most people. In any case, the many different ways in which the word normal has been used over the centuries have made man less, rather than more, certain about himself. This is related to the fact that we are still limited in our understanding of human sexuality and that we are only slowly pushing back the darkness that has shrouded so much of man's behavior.

When our knowledge is partial, we all tend to interpret what we observe according to our own needs. These, of course, can be given their pattern in a wide variety of ways. We all grind our axes differently in the cause of defending a viewpoint in which we ourselves are emotionally invested. Perhaps this confusion is one of the reasons that the average man so often speaks about sexuality in a joking manner. There are those who would draw great morals from man's tendency to make jokes about serious aspects of sexuality, saying that this indicates his lack of respect for it or his failure to appreciate womankind, or something else like that. I think rather that we use humor because the business of sexuality, which has so many implications for our own self-understanding, is still heavily weighted with threat for the common man. Humor gives us an easy way to express our anxiety about sexual conflicts; it makes them less oppressive and less crowding of the self. It is one of the signs that we are not quite as confident in our knowledge about sex as we would like to believe. There is, in fact, something genuinely foreboding about the individual who can never smile or be playful about the subject of sexuality.

Research on sexuality has increased over recent years but much of it is fragmentary and little of it has been carefully checked or replicated by other researchers. There is a myth connected with the word research, however, which says that if you can use it in a sentence you enhance your credibility enormously. Research is one of the favorite myths of Americans who spend a great deal of money on it without promising to pay strict attention to the results. People go on doing things pretty much the way they want even after they have paid expensive consultants large fees in order to tell them how to do things in a better fashion. Perhaps the classic example of our age is found in the Pentagon papers where the laboriously gathered advice of the CIA on the possible alternatives in Vietnam has turned out to have been exactly correct in so many instances and to have been totally ignored by the officials for whom the information was gathered. So it is with sexuality. The myths persist despite research findings, except that these myths now seem enhanced by the very fact that research has been done on sex. It is as though the myths took strength from the very research which tended to disprove them. Marriage manuals offer us some of the best examples of the enhancement of myths with the aura of research. This has been true as long as marriage manuals have been written. In fact, a comparison of the marriage manuals of a century ago with those currently popular is most instructive in this regard. It may be that a century from now we will look back on our contemporary manuals and judge them to be as quaint and conservative as those of the last century now seem to us. Their perusal is a caution for any man who thinks that we are in full command of our understanding of sex or marriage.

A century ago marriage manuals emphasized a rationally ordered life; spontaneity was to be bound down by restraint. The quality needed most by a woman was that of being industrious, although she was also praised in her marital role for possessing a spirit of reverence, obedience, and submission. Love was presented more as the product rather than as the motivation for marriage. The young couple were urged to keep up with modern science, especially insofar as the then-available research shed light on the relationship between the sexes. To this end, for example, man and woman were encouraged to study phrenology, the then-popular science that analyzed personality according to the contours of the head. Sex was not mentioned very much and only in tightly restrained tones; even then sex was caught in a not unfamiliar web of mythology. The married couple were told, for exam-

ple, that healthier children would come from intercourse
in the morning when the man and woman felt most
vigorous. A minority of authors urged a broadened understanding of sex, perhaps preparing the way for the time
when sexual activity could be considered in terms other
than those of procreation. There was little evidence, however, of any effort to redefine the role of women in society. ("Mate Choice and Domestic Life in the 19th
Century Marriage Manual" by Michael Gordon and
M. Charles Bernstein, *The Journal of Marriage and the
Family*, November 1970, pp. 665–74.)

In the marriage manuals of this century we have a re-
versal of many of the pieces of advice given out so
solemnly to our ancestors. Love, of course, is what brings
people to marriage; the idealization of this romantic love
is emphasized in contemporary discussions of sex. In fact,
present-day manuals of marriage discuss sex almost to the
exclusion of other issues. The ideal is no longer a studied
rationality but a ready spontaneity in married life, which
is to say, according to present manuals, the sexual life of
the couple.

This illustrates one of the major inconsistencies that suggests that we are not as integrated or self-confident sexually as we would like to appear. While the experts no
longer suggest the study of phrenology, they have un-
limited suggestions about sexual technique; they go raptur-
ous as they describe the myth of the perfect and hopefully
simultaneous orgasm. Indeed, one cannot read contemporary marriage manuals without sensing the enormous
burden that has been put on the man for the successful
understanding, initiation, and carrying through of sexual
relations which are, if at all possible, to be successively
more spectacular. This myth, with even less scientific basis
than phrenology, is a staple of the modern marriage books;
although there are obviously some exceptions to this, the
married couple are urged to make the trophy of simultaneous orgasm the goal of their experience of marital
sex. Sex, in at least some of the manuals, is clearly distinguished from procreational activity; it is defined as rec-

reational activity, a kind of having fun with sex that is the mark of the twentieth-century sophisticate. Never have so many people been told to have so much fun with sex in such a rigid and dogmatic way. It is difficult to see how, burdened with dotted-line directions about achieving a mythical ideal, a young couple would not feel quite self-conscious and awkward in their efforts to be "spontaneous" in the way the sex experts have instructed them. This clear but subtle rationality differs little from that of the century-old manuals as the enthusiastic advisers of today program the couple for spontaneous sex. It is hardly surprising that people are continually intimidated about sexuality; they are willing to believe and try anything that looks sexually promising even as the internal contradictions of the sexual advice are covered by the syrupy voices of the experts.

Yet the marriage manuals sell in great numbers; they are a response to man's search for a better understanding of himself and his sexuality. They are books bought by people who are uncertain and who almost desperately need some kind of reassurance and authoritative help. Unfortunately, much of the advice that man gets now is not a great improvement over the advice he got a hundred years ago. In the area of sexuality, the traditional ideal of the man of science who is also a man of integrity is genuinely needed. He is humble before his investigations, qualified in his interpretations of his results, and not immediately an evangelist or a philosopher on the basis of incomplete information.

Seeming to be knowledgeable about sexuality is, for most Americans, a bluff pose which, with the constantly taxed poise of the Great Impostor, they try to carry off throughout a lifetime. The public anxiety about sex is just the visible edge of the crippling fear which has fed so long and so lustily on ignorance. Lionel Trilling, the essayist, in commenting on the impact of Kinsey's research, observed, "Nothing shows more clearly the extent to which modern society has atomized itself than the isolation in sexual ignorance which exists among us. . . . Many cultures, the most primitive and the most complex, have entertained sexual fears of an irrational sort, but probably our culture is unique in strictly isolating the individual in the fears that society has devised." (Lionel Trilling, *The Liberal Imagination,* Garden City, Doubleday & Company, Inc., Anchor Books, 1953, p. 16.) This substratum of uninstructed fear makes men continuously vulnerable to rumor, gossip, and the latest edition of the sexual myths. It is clear that men cannot solve their problems about sexuality by concentrating on them alone, or by isolating them from the general context of personal development. Whenever the pressures in a society prevent people from dealing more straightforwardly with sex, this kind of distorted outcome occurs: Human beings are constantly preoccupied with the sexuality but they make only minimal progress in understanding and integrating it into their lives because of the inhibiting emotional climate which constricts them and their capacity to place sex into the overall map of personality. In other words, it is not merely an openness to the questions of sex that is needed; there is a far more urgent need for an overall openness to man.

Curiously enough, some of the greatest advocates of sexual freedom and the dissemination of sexually related information are quite unwilling to enlarge their focus to include other aspects of human experience. The religious nature and needs of the person are, for example, seldom discussed in the effort to help man get himself together sexually. Religion is written off as one of the sources of man's enslavement to sexual ignorance. While there have been unfortunate pronouncements about man and his sexuality on the part of certain religious leaders at different times in history, this does not lessen the significance of man's religious longings, nor eliminate the need for weighing them in the scale on which we attempt to help man achieve his balance. In other words, man cannot get himself together just sexually; he can only do it humanly, by pursuing a deeper and richer understanding of all that he is as a person. Only then, when he has learned, for example, why he settles for half-truths about his sexuality, will he find himself on the other side of the fear that frustrates his development. He will never, however, unlock the mysteries of his sexuality by concentrating intently and exclusively on them; that is part of the problem right now. Understanding human sexuality is a complex problem that simply cannot be solved by quick and easy methods. All the generations of myth have made this promise to man—that the way is simple to sexual self-understanding, and that all the kingdoms will be his if he falls down and accepts their absolutes.

But human growth and the richness of sexual experience are never successfully summarized under a fashionable code that shifts with the seasons. Man must be understood and appreciated with more compassion than judgment and with a greater willingness to free him rather than to control him. The first lesson remains that we have more yet to learn than we already know and that man must be approached in his totality rather than section by section if he is to mature sexually. As Simon and Gagnon have said about human behavior, ". . . it is without an absolutely predetermined and fixed shape and content, and it is a complex condition which derives from man's unique abilities to think, act, and remember and his need to live with other humans." (William Simon and John H. Gagnon, *Sexual Deviance*, New York, Harper & Row, 1967, p. 282.)

Man is still searching out an understanding of his sexuality. The individual can, however, take basic soundings of it to judge whether it is in the context of a relationship that gives it significance as an exchange between persons who prize and love each other. Beyond that his information is far from exhaustive. The prophets who present themselves with all the answers, the self-styled philosophers who market reassurance: These are the makers of the worst of the current myths, the idea that we know everything we should know about sex. It is a myth with a leading man and woman, the supremely self-confident male and female. But it is a myth, and a cruel one at that. No one is exempt, not even the healthiest of us, from certain

fears and doubts about ourselves. These are only sub-
sumed and worked through in the context of a human
relationship in which sexuality is gradually integrated into
a total pattern of personal identity. We do not yet know
everything about sex but we do know something; and that
something tells us that man is on the right track when he
reaches through his sexuality to those he loves, when he
lives as a sexual rather than just as a genital person. The
highest measure of a loving person's compassion is his
willingness patiently to understand rather than quickly to
judge the perplexing problems of a world that grows wise
very slowly.

11
THE GAY MYTH

Our information about sexual deviance is, in the kindest possible judgment, less than adequate, and yet there is no subject about which there are stronger and noisier convictions or more energetic claims to final wisdom. Just living and breathing in a culture that makes so many cruel and uneasy jokes about sexual deviance convinces that powerful tides of uneasiness wash across our corporate psyche on this subject. If we are puzzled by sexuality in general, we are absolutely overwhelmed by deviant sexuality in particular. But men cannot leave the topic nor those who experience sexual deviation alone; this tireless and anxious concern is just another surface quiver that tells of man's age-old struggles around this subject. It is, in fact, difficult to speak about problems of sexual deviation in a calm and intelligent way even today. Of all subjects, the present state of our ignorance about sexual deviance should convince us that we are far from a full understanding of human sexuality even today. When we can approach this subject with just a little more confidence that we will not be consumed by it, we will have taken a large and significant step toward individual and collective sexual maturity.

At the present moment, however, we are just edging toward this goal; the more open talk about homosexuality, for example, and its gradual incorporation into American

cultural consciousness are not free of strong emotional
impact. Homosexuality is probably the most obvious example of those attitudes and behavior which we classify as
deviant. This latter term is at least a step forward from
the blanket term *perversion* which was formerly applied
quite freely to all the mutations of sexual development.
That judgmental word was, of course, a part of the old
myth that cast homosexuals into villainous roles and made
them silent and unapproachable outcasts from ordinary
society. The new myths tell us that gay is good or even
better than straight sexuality, that it is everything from a
solution to overpopulation to the finest bloom of human
friendship. Neither of these myths tells any of us the truth;
they are extreme positions that make it difficult to inspect
that large middle ground on which we will find the fullest
understanding of all sexual questions.

Sexual deviance and homosexuality, in particular, have
a new visibility, but it is still true that most persons find
it difficult to maintain an open and unprejudiced attitude
toward the phenomenon of homosexuality. That is why
many Gay Liberationists are looked on as entertainment
rather than taken seriously as human beings. Homosexuality as a word bears the weight of so many connotations
that it can hardly be used unless one is willing to define
quite carefully the behavior or attitudes to which one refers. Homosexuality has been variously called a sin and
a sickness on the one hand and on the other, the highest
form of love and friendship. It can, according to clinical
reports, refer to lifetime patterns of deeply ingrained and
debilitating personality attitudes and behaviors; it can also
refer to what seem to be transient states in the development
of normal persons toward the commonly accepted goal of
full heterosexuality. Homosexuality can frighten the life
out of fairly average people as it emerges from the deep
sea of their own impulses and fantasies to surprise them
and raise the question which has become such a frightening one in contemporary America: "Am I a homosexual?"
This question, of course, merely reflects in another way the
widespread concern about sexual adequacy which is found

in a large proportion of adults. The worry about homosexuality in American culture has, however, intensified both the difficulty in discussing it objectively as well as the scientific efforts to put together some mosaic of understanding out of the scraps of evidence at hand.

The discussion of sexual deviation is handicapped by the fact that there has been a long history of equating deviant behaviors with sin. Theologians now have difficulty in saying which, if any, things are intrinsically sinful; and it is clear that such factors as intention, circumstances, and consequences define sinfulness more than the objective nature of the action under consideration. In any case, there has been a strong emotional reaction against homosexuality on the part of many people; this feeling, which many of them would identify as almost natural, despite all that we have learned, is still very strong today. Even many professionals who must work with homosexuals find that they are uneasy about doing this; they sense the negative shading of their outlook that occurs when they perceive another person as homosexual. This and similar manifestations of spontaneous outrage at homosexuality suggest that the defense mechanism of reaction-formation is at work in the lives of many people who react in this manner. Because they fear the possibility of homosexuality in themselves or because they have even experienced some homosexual impulses at one time or another, they experience a threat to their "normal" picture of themselves. The phenomenon of excessive outrage against the homosexual is, according to many observers, the device by which some individuals muffle their own uneasiness. After all, the man who is hunting down the perfect orgasm cannot but be struck paralyzed with fear at the notion that he might harbor some homosexual feelings within himself. Science also tells us, of course, that most relatively well-adjusted people experience homosexual feelings at least occasionally in their lives. What is astounding is the incredible fear that has been associated with homosexuality and the strong hostile feelings which are raised in reaction to its presence.

As far as sexual deviations go, our knowledge is far from unified or complete. We do know that sexual problems appear in disguised forms during a period when society deals with persons in heavily repressive ways. A study of the history of sexuality shows how what we term its deviant manifestations are linked with the overall cultural environment. Psychiatrist Judd Marmor, in a recent article, has shown the correlation between societal events and the various manifestations of sexual difficulties:

> There is no way in which the concepts of normal and deviant sexual behavior can be divorced from the value systems of our society; and since such value systems are always in the process of evolution and change, we must be prepared to face the possibility that some patterns currently considered deviant may not always be so regarded. The fact that we now refer to sexual "deviations" rather than to "perversions" already represents an evolutionary change within our culture toward a more objective and scientific approach to these problems, in contrast to the highly moralistic and pejorative approach of the previous generation. (*The Journal of the American Medical Association*, July 12, 1971, Vol. 217, No. 2, p. 169.)

Man's history is indeed complicated; only great sensitivity to man's reactions in differing environments and differing historical situations can help us to understand what we call sexual deviations in their proper perspective. Homosexuality, for example, has had a varied history, exalted and written into the law of the land in Sparta, and considered the unspeakable crime in turn-of-the-century England. The truth about homosexuality may ultimately be understood only when we can look deeply into the historical patterns, the prevailing values, and the motivations for certain beliefs held by society at different times in history. We do not know enough about any of these things. The best scientific wisdom tells us that there is a great deal more to know before we can say the last word on homosexuality. While it seems neither to be a grace nor an illness, it is still difficult to get it into focus as a dynamic human problem.

There is remarkably little research on homosexuality, although there are many theories about its origin. Some of these look for genetic determinants, for inherited problems in hormonal balance, or for some short-circuit in a central coding section of the brain. Many others interpret homosexual behavior as the psychological outcome of faulted patterns of family life. One reality that is reliable, however, is the enormity of the suffering that has been experienced by human beings around the subject of homosexuals. In a recent analysis and replication of Bieber's (*Homosexuality: A Psychoanalytic Study*, New York, Basic Books, 1962) related homosexuality to the familial combination of a passive and ineffectual father with a close-binding and dominating mother. These findings have been reproduced in other small-scale researches on the subject; they have also been validated in the clinical experience of many therapists who have worked with homosexuals. In a recent analysis and replication of Bieber's work, Ray B. Arens, Associate Professor of Psychiatry at Loma Linda University School of Medicine in California, suggested that the emphasis on the role of the parents neglects to include the role of the child himself in eliciting certain kinds of behavior from his parents. He writes:

Some consideration must be given to the likelihood that the child's inner characteristics at least partially determine parental reactions and attitudes toward him. For instance, it is just as tenable to assume that the father of a pre-homosexual son becomes detached or hostile because he does not understand his son, is disappointed in him, or threatened by him, as it is to assume that the son becomes homosexual because of the father's rejection. (*Medical Aspects of Human Sexuality*, April 1971, p. 176.)

Arens does not disagree with the fact that family patterns are important in giving rise to homosexuality. He does, however, indicate that no simple equation can be written to explain homosexual development and that the best thing science can do is proceed slowly and carefully as it tries to dissipate the clouds of darkness that still shroud our full understanding of homosexuality.

On the other side, there are repeated assertions that homosexuality is a natural variant, perhaps even a preferred variant, of human sexual experience, and that it ranks with heterosexuality as a manifestation of human development. This is the kind of assertion, again not backed by very much scientific evidence, that the homosexual presents to explain his way of life. There is a slightly tortured quality to some of these hymns to homosexuality; what these exaltations of homosexuality mean in the whole panorama of human growth is by no means clear.

It is obvious, however, that something is happening in society at the present time, some softening of the defensive fibers that has let homosexuality emerge into the daylight more fully than it ever has in American social history. The homosexual is far from being accepted but he is certainly allowed to exist, socialize, and entertain himself with increased freedom, at least in the large and absorbent metropolitan areas. This does not make homosexuality into a model way of life, but it at least permits the rest of the world to see and perhaps understand the living problems of homosexuals. Perhaps it indicates that men in general are coming closer to dealing with their own homosexual impulses in other than suppressive ways. This outcome could only be helpful because it would remove much of the lingering fear that dances like magnetic forces around the field of human sexual impulses. When men can face with less fear the complex of feelings and impulses that are part of each person's sexuality, they will be able to accept and integrate their experience into a less prejudiced and more creative self-identity. That is to say, when persons can be more friendly toward what really goes on inside them, they will feel less pressure to deny or distort their experience of themselves; the achievement of their masculine or feminine identity will be less the acceptance of a rigidly imposed social stereotype and more the attainment of a multidimensioned truth about themselves.

Greater openness to self can only increase our chances of more successful gender identity.

This is by no means to endorse homosexual behavior nor to accept the oversimplified myth that gay is good. The recent evidence supplied by psychiatrist Laurence Hatterer of the overwhelming desire on the part of homosexual men, were they to be fathers, to see their sons free of this problem is enough to make anybody pause in making that judgment. I think, however, that we have to come to look beneath the sexual behavior to the questions, many of them not fully answered, which center on the personality dynamics of individual homosexuals and the significance of homosexual activity in their lives. To take but one example, is it really too horrendous to believe that a homosexual may, according to the modality of his sexual adjustment, be reaching successfully out of himself and toward another person in his sexual activity? Is it not possible that his effort to move out of himself and toward the other is the difficult-to-read sign of genuine growth on his part? In other words, homosexual activity, even if it is not human expression at full term, may be forward movement for the lonely and isolated individual who breaks out of his own narcissistic self-concern. Obviously, knowing the exploitative possibilities in all sexual relationships, one could only make a judgment on this in individual cases. But the Christian must begin to look at homosexuality with this kind of sensitivity rather than with the overmasculinized disgust that prevents him from ever inspecting it closely at all. Heterosexuals, after all, have the same basic challenge to break free of their own self-absorption in their sexual relationships, and their potential for selfishness and exploitation is just as great as that of the homosexual. Indeed, if the evidence suggesting that homosexuality arises in families where there is a faulted marital relationship between man and woman is even partially correct, then heterosexuals have an obligation to improve their relationships rather than to reject the homosexuality which they have, through their failed masculinity and femininity, caused to exist.

Society, however, still has enormous difficulties in understanding homosexuality; it is tempted either to exalt or to damn it, in fact, to Goddamn it; society is frightened by it in its own innards, and it has proceeded very slowly to collect reliable scientific information about it. We do not know enough to pretend to be absolutely wise on this or many other aspects of human sexual behavior. There will be no unraveling of our attitudes toward sexual deviation or what we presume to be healthy sexual expression unless we are willing to examine more closely the values that underpin these decisions.

To examine our values in depth is an achingly difficult task. We are, after all, so easily caught up on one side or the other because of the acquired prejudices and myths that make human beings both interesting and confusing. This goes well beyond the question of sexual behaviors, of course, and includes everything from warfare to Women's Lib. In an age in which confrontation has become a key word, at a time when our ears still ring with the curses and taunts that cry of man's multiplied frustrations, we are all edgily aware that quiet discussions of disputed points are almost a thing of the past. It is not an easy thing for a man to ask what he believes in and why; it is painful to look at our own self-inflicted wounds and to realize how easily we can deceive ourselves; it is uncomfortable to discover that many of the things we say we believe freely and nobly are things we have to hold on to because of our own psychological needs. In no area of our lives is this more true than the sexual. But richer wisdom is denied to those who are afraid to uncover their own prejudices and inadequacies. It is a long journey for all of us, one that will surely be made only slowly through the coming generations; and yet it must be made if we are to replace rumor and myth with something like wisdom about human sexuality.

The fundamental question concerns what we believe about man. It is difficult to sustain any viewpoint on deviance or health unless one works through some convictions about the nature of the person. Without some philosophy or theology that deals sensitively with the realities of human experience, a man must either surrender to the tyranny of myth or the tyranny of authoritarian persons who will make the decisions about all of life's values. At the present time there are many who quite unconsciously give themselves over to the domination of one or the other of these forces, to the mythologizers or the sexual fascists. No satisfactory response to the problem of sexual deviation will ever come separate from a unified philosophy and psychology of man; for only with these can a man take true responsibility for himself.

The question of healthy and unhealthy sexuality causes us to confront our beliefs about the most important values in a man's life. The inheritor of the Judeo-Christian tradition cannot easily or for long commit himself, for example, to a moral yardstick as simple as pleasure without coming into conflict with the ideals of his heritage. The modern world has, of course, seen many people put aside this very tradition of beliefs in the name of becoming liberated sexually. They have felt weighed down by the distortions of this tradition which were introduced into it over the years. The solution, however, is not to abandon all systems of religious belief, but to purify them, and to search for a more solid faith on which to base contemporary experience and judgment. Man cannot survive long without some system of beliefs by which he forms his decisions about his actions and behavior; he soon becomes marginal and alienated, unhealed by the formless atmosphere of his new freedom. This is precisely the ambiance that is being created by the new mythology of sex; it says that sex is indifferent in human exchange and that we can move unhindered toward the experiences that gratify us. This cruel myth sunders man's last threads of connection with the meaning of the kind of love which illumines the meaning of life for him as it cracks the shell of his self-containment. And no problem about sex, healthy or unhealthy, will ever be understood or responded to sensitively except by those persons who have first learned the perennially difficult lessons of loving. It is only in the light of

what love tells us about what we do with and to others that
we achieve the moral maturity that enables us to deal with
all sexual questions in a more compassionate and enlightened way.

The question we come to concerns our grasp of and
capacity for real love. That is the measure urged on us by
the situationists, but it is neither simple nor easy to apply
it to the intimate sexual exchanges in which we are so willing to rationalize our behavior. As far as sexual deviation goes, it is even more difficult to apply this standard,
and one must, as in other human situations, give high
marks to the person who is earnestly trying to love another
rather than just submerge more deeply into the coils of
himself. All men spend most of their lives learning how to
love; it is not a challenge that comes only to heterosexuals
or homosexuals. It is, as a matter of fact, a challenge that
is more a goal than a reality for the majority of us. We
are, as a people, only beginning to understand ourselves,
but we are still rooted deeply in self-concern and very far
as yet from the kind of awareness that we will possess
when we have mastered better the meaning of human love.
Love dictates that we be presently open to learning more
about all sexual manifestations and that we are not ready
to write or utter the last word of judgment yet. We must
use the light that we have to look with compassion and
understanding on ourselves and our struggles to be human. But that does not mean that we have to embrace
sexual deviation as an ideal any more than we embrace
adultery as an ideal in human relationships; it means that
we need more light to understand ourselves, and that dis-
ciplined love is its best source for us. It is the measure that
enables us to tell the difference between what is healthy
and unhealthy in our exchanges with each other.

What, then, can be said about the presence or absence
of health in human sexual behavior? Or is the prevailing
wisdom in the myth that everything is normal or at least a
matter of indifference? We are not quite so bereft of guide-
lines as one might suppose. Although our exact knowledge
about certain aspects of sexuality is limited, what we do

know allows us to make some conclusion about the difference between healthy and unhealthy human attitudes. A lack of complete scientific information does not make total relativism the only alternative. And love is not a shapeless sentimental mass in whose shadow we freely do anything we please. We can say something about sexual behavior that matches man's human possibilities, that is, in other words, healthy for the growing person. Marmor points out that habitual and preferential use of non-genital outlets for sexual release, especially when this becomes an end in itself, suggests "almost always, in the context of our culture . . . some disturbance in personality functioning." (Loc. cit.) He also identifies other categories of sexual behavior which are recognized by most scientific observers as primitive and as major signs of a lack of personality development. While these manifestations must be approached compassionately by scientists, they cannot be designated as of little or no significance in the sexual behavior of the individual. These include sexual activities with immature partners of either sex, with animals, with dead people, or with inanimate objects. You just cannot say that these things make no difference.

We can surely go beyond the definition of extreme forms of sexual deviation, however, to examine the qualities of sexual behavior which reveal whether they are innately healthy or not. Common sense is not the least of our allies in making these judgments. Common sense is the capacity we retain to tell the difference between what is healthy and what is not. When a person is too immature to possess a store of common sense then he will have difficulty doing this. If we cannot rely on a well-developed sense of judgment about this in true adults, then human sexual expression would be a tangled mess beyond the comprehension of any of us. There are, however, certain values which are perceived across the boundaries of cultures; these are regarded as symbolic of man in his highest moment of mature self-realization. Not the least of these centers on his sexual behavior.

For example, human sexual activity that is effectively

divorced from human relationships loses a quality that makes a considerable difference in the meaning of the sexual experience itself. When sexuality is part of a relationship that expresses genuine liking and responsible love between persons, then it potently reinforces, by its own depth, an already deep reality. When sex is used to express interpersonal guilt, hate, or some other form of hostility, when it expresses boiling emotions in one person that are not related to the other, then the whole action is unhealthy or at least a sign of a lack of full personal development. As Marmor notes:

> Healthy sexuality seeks erotic pleasure in the context of tenderness and affection; pathologic sexuality is motivated by needs for reassurance or relief from non-sexual sources of tension. Healthy sexuality seeks both to give and receive pleasure; neurotic forms are unbalanced towards excessive giving or taking. Healthy sexuality is discriminating as to partners; neurotic patterns often tend to be non-discriminating. The periodicity of healthy sexuality is determined primarily by recurrent erotic tensions in the context of affection. Neurotic sexual drives, on the other hand, are triggered less by the erotic needs than by non-erotic tensions and therefore more apt to be compulsive in their patterns of occurrence. (Op. cit. p. 170.)

In the long run, what is healthy holds together across every field of human experience; you simply cannot separate out one aspect of what man does and make all your judgments through focusing on that alone. That is exactly the difficulty that arises when sexuality is torn out of the larger background of human experience of which it is admittedly a significant but not autonomous part. If there is a continuity in what is humanly healthy, the same ring to all the coins of our transactions, then the best index of healthy sexuality may be in the character of all the associated actions of our lives. A man cannot, for example, be religiously healthy—a man of genuine concern for others —and personally selfish at the same time. There is something wrong with what he calls religion if this is the case. So, too, the man who wants to pass judgment on whether his sexual life is one marked by some effort to give generously to another might well inspect the rest of his life to discover the overall quality of his sharing of himself with others; he cannot successfully separate his sexual activity from his human activity. They have the same source in his person and it is unlikely that one will reflect a truly loving attitude toward life if the other does not. We must, in other words, place our sexuality into the broader context of our total lives and not be deceived by the myths that make what we do sexually irrelevant to what we are as men and women. Only when we take our sexuality that seriously will we be freed from the myths that make it so difficult even to think about subjects like homosexuality with clarity and compassion. Ultimately, when we are older and wiser, we will understand the profound link between healthy sexuality and loving personality, and we will recognize the pale distortions that sell man out too short and too quickly as an agent of instant pleasure or indifferent behavior.

What possible conclusions can a person come to about the subject of deviant sexuality? First, that we are at the beginning stages of understanding it, and that it is a complex phenomenon that beggars facile description or judgment. Secondly, our ability to deal constructively with the questions of sexual deviation will vary in proportion to our openness to our inner human experience; the more we can put aside fear and look carefully at the montage of elements that are the raw material of eventual sexual maturity the less constrained we will be to live by unexamined stereotypes. The more we are able to understand our own sexual experience the more freely and fully will we achieve healthy gender identity; the signs of our growing sensitivity to this are already appearing in the arts and other aspects of our cultural behavior. Thirdly, the polarized myths of the *he-man freak* and the *gay is better* will disintegrate as we become more comfortable with a deeper understanding of our masculine and feminine identities.

Fourthly, we are not helpless to make judgments about what constitutes healthy and unhealthy sexual behavior; the same standards of what makes for any kind of loving behavior may be applied to sexual experience, and sensible and trustworthy judgments can be made. This is a difficult task, however, that demands more complete overall growth if it is to be achieved with integrity; but only the most amorphous personality can hold for the relative indifference of all sexual behavior. Fifthly, the separation of sexuality from the context of human personality in the discussion of deviations merely makes the task of compassionate understanding of human development more difficult.

12

THE "AMERICA THE DEPRAVED" MYTH

Perhaps few societies have been so preoccupied with sex as the American, but neither have many societies tried to integrate the experiences of love and marriage in a systematic way. America, whose citizens are so fond of self-examination and national breast-beating, cannot be totally indicted as depraved even by those who most bemoan its sexual failings or its other national blemishes. The sex that permeates American life today is symbolic, and to some extent prophetic, and there is the possibility that, despite the well-publicized and well-documented contemporary sexual hang-ups, something better in our understanding of sex and something richer in our understanding of the person may emerge from it all. The outcome of the current boiling situation, like the pot of a cook who isn't quite sure of what he is up to despite his good instincts, is still in doubt. Americans are struggling with sex; they are confused, immature, and beset with myths, but they are trying to put things together truthfully. The possibility remains that a more profound and human sexual ethic may yet come from, of all places, America. Our sexual tomorrow may not be totally golden, but it will not be just the night.

America is neither supersophisticated nor totally depraved. The two-headed myth must be slain if we are to understand that the current conflict about the nature and role of men and women might give rise to a finer and more subtle understanding of human sexuality. First, the myth that we are sexually sophisticated. America is not, of course, sailing fearlessly and directly down the right track in the current explosion of erotic confusion. Americans are very optimistic about it, however. The quick, easy, and well-publicized answers that come out almost monthly to soothe the sexual quirks of the average Americans are simply too glib and immature to pass for long-lasting wisdom. But middle-class America buys the answers masterfully rewritten for every audience from the put-on sex of *Cosmopolitan* to the wonderfully middle-brow "new hope for your sex life" pieces in the *Reader's Digest*. The mentality that we can approach and cure problems as complex as those associated with sexual conflicts is characteristically American. We have solved problems successfully in the area of technological production so it is only logical to believe that, given the money and the ingenuity, we can come up with a crash program for sex as well. Rotarian enthusiasm and keen-minded engineers, however, do not make the business of growing up any easier. The redemption of sex is well beyond the limits of this mythical attitude.

The other and uglier head of the myth portrays Americans as sexually bold and inventive predators on the North American continent, thinking of nothing else but sexual conquest and lusting in their tents when they are not busy on their pilgrimages of rape and ruin. This is the picture that appeals to those who have the Roman Empire-complex myth. This latter myth allows some pessimist to look at the world and compare everything he sees with the decline and fall of that long-gone civilization. The pages of contemporary observation, many of them on something less than the sure footing of scholarship, see the sexual preoccupation of Americans as one of the large signs of a culture that is cracking and about to fall into a dusty pile of barbecue pits and TV antennae. This is easy caricature; America is thus Amerika. Nonetheless, there are signs that America, despite its relatively short history, has pushed its roots more deeply into the soil and is showing signs of growing more mature.

Americans have always been able to face the truth, especially when it hurts them, and then to try to do something about it. As a country, the United States has recently had to redefine some of its most enduring myths, as, for example, that of uncomplicated patriotism and idealized democracy. Americans have done this, however, without yet destroying themselves despite the incredible ruptures in the culture which have been caused by the Vietnam War. The pain of it has been good for the American soul. A country grown suddenly more aware of its limitations and the fact that raw power and wealth cannot of themselves achieve a desired end has learned a lot from history; it demonstrates a vitality to adjust itself to the truth that has few parallels in any other part of the world. Other countries have learned different ways of dealing with the truth, especially with truths which are disturbing to them and which they would rather hide from themselves than deal with directly. Some European countries which are strongly critical of the United States are not exactly models of openness in dealing with the truth about themselves. Americans have never thought that fighting duels did anything but obscure the truth that was disputed in the first place.

When America is able to look beneath the present publicity and the almost hysterical tone of discussions about sex, it will face truths that may be as difficult as those which it has learned through senseless wars, but they will be just as good for its soul. The most important discovery is that there is a lot of anxiety beneath the bluster and that much of this centers on the American masculine insecurity about himself. This has been heightened by the newly verbalized challenge of Women's Lib to do battle on more nearly equal grounds and it is also complicated by a variety of other cultural problems. It is important to review some of the aspects of the American man's shaky self-confidence. A survey of the sexual lives of Americans would surely reveal that many of them are far from high powered and that, although a good deal of fantasy life may be devoted to erotic longings, many Americans, especially males, are deeply troubled by the ancient specter that never tires of challenging them to prove themselves as card-carrying, female-orgasm-causing heterosexuals. The typical American male falters understandably under the burden of sexual expectations which has been placed on his shoulders by the amateur sexologists, marriage-manual writers, and other minor poets of the sexual revolution. He goes along with it all because of the terrible fear that others might discover that he is less than the proud and knowledgeable bull that mythology makes of him. A closer look reveals not only a wrinkled brow but a complex of symptoms that suggests that the average American is weary of trying to be supermale.

One must examine, for example, and despite all the talk about premarital sex, the number of marriages that are not consummated for varying periods of time after the wedding ceremony is performed. While the awkward problems are seldom discussed publicly, the reasons for the difficulties, which are ordinarily psychological rather than physiological, reflect the crippling uncertainties which affect the lives of many contemporary Americans. Lack of consummation is not a rare difficulty; it is also in most cases, a treatable one. It is a scourge because people who suffer from it are frequently so upset by it that they do not seek proper help; sometimes they seek it in such indirect terms that the physician or person from whom they seek it never does understand what they are talking about. (For a detailed study of this problem, see L. J. Freedman, *Virgin Wives: A Study of Unconsummated Marriage*, London, Tavistock Publishers Ltd., 1962.)

There are also many marriages which grow gradually sexless, that is, marital unions in which sexual intercourse between the husband and wife diminishes markedly as the years go by. There are some marriages, as we have always known, in which sex plays a relatively minor part. People can marry for appearances, as well as for many other reasons which make the exclusion of sex a convenience for both partners. Many of these marriages exist, and although the men and women in some of them find compensating sexual experience in relationships outside the marriage, it is not uncommon to find that their sexual lives are actually quite muted. Here again the reasons are mainly psychological. Boredom with routine, failure to maintain the health of the interpersonal relationship of the husband and wife, and such random things as fears about one's continued health after an illness or childbirth: All of these can be factors in the marriage in which sex has died. It has been observed that the late-night talk shows on television have provided a convenient bridge to a night's sleep across which the partners who wish to avoid sex relations may walk rather easily. It was no joke when Johnny Carson said of his and other late-night talk shows, "We're more effective than birth-control pills." (*Time* magazine, May 19, 1967.) In a recent article, psychiatrist Alfred Auerback states, "Probably one of the most useful functions of late late TV programs is to ease the coexistence of spouses who are bored with each other, who no longer really enjoy each other's companionship and, in particular, the sexual relationship." (*Medical Aspects of Human Sexuality,* January 1970, p. 36.) TV has merely added itself to the long list of "avoidance mechanisms" with which men and women have been familiar for generations. Although Americans are presumably bent on sexual experience at every opportunity, there are many situations, especially those relationships that have lost their vitality, in which this is simply not so.

Psychiatrist Ralph R. Greenson of the UCLA School of Medicine has also written recently about an increase in what he terms "sexual apathy" in men. In *California Medicine* he notes an increased sexual boredom in the middle-aged as well as an increase in the efforts of these men to substitute something else for the constant testing of themselves, which they feel sex has come to be. He sees these and other signs in his clinical practice as evidence that men are presently acting out their unconscious fear of women in an increasingly serious way. Greenson suggests that an important factor is the increase in hostility and fear between the sexes, above all in men, which seems to have mounted with the increasing ascendancy of women. As women in our society have become more assertive and daring, men seem to have become more passive and timid in life in general, and particularly in sexual matters. Men are moving back toward a more secure position, behind the lines where they can successfully separate the notion of sexual experience from human relationships. This is the dynamic of sexual apathy, a movement away from the human context which is the necessary setting for rich sexual experience. "Loving is risk taking," Greenson writes. "It implies daring to be vulnerable and hurt. In this sense, the search for security is the enemy of loving and in our society the emphasis is on security. One of these results of this attitude is the putting off of love from sex and consequently we so frequently find love without passion and sex without emotional involvement."

While it is obvious that these observations hardly justify the conclusion that we are witnessing a major trend in the behavior of American males, many clinicians would agree that Americans with these problems enter their offices every week. These signs of sexual uncertainty are, after all, only the same realities that have been written about by our poets and novelists. The wrenching tales of sexual human beings under pressure who want to look good even though they are increasingly weary and filled with feelings of oppression. The American scene is neither sophisticated nor depraved; it is filled with frightened and uncertain people who do not understand themselves or their sexuality very well.

There is no doubt that women have evidenced an increasing sense of sureness about themselves and that this has contributed to the crack in the surface confidence of the American male. American women, especially in their liberation movement, although rattling with a defensive kind of hostility, have reasserted themselves anew. The American woman will not accept the passive role any longer; she has made a point of the fact that she no longer believes the myth that she must live out this role in sexual relationships. This new American woman has driven the old American man up the wall on which his cherished myth of superiority was scrawled. This has been in the context of seeking generalized equality with men, but her battle cries have sent shivers down the spines of some of our most hairy-chested male spokesmen. The precipitate of this chemistry of intersex conflict is fear, according to some, a fear that may have been hidden in man's unconscious for a long time, a fear that even now is verbalized only partially. Tension mounts between man and woman in contemporary American society and the male, as if he did not have enough problems already, is being pushed toward redefining himself and the parameters of his own masculinity. The American male hardly sounds depraved but he does sound on the spot, and despite the fiery fallout of the American woman's new surge for full rights, a better relationship of man and woman may come from this conflict.

Americans, who have always tried to associate love and marriage, are not as set in their ways as many of the other peoples of the world. They have not, as have many males elsewhere, sold out for a mistress-wife fiction that amounts to active polygamy. They have tried, failing as often as they have succeeded, to make marriage work and to have it carried forward by the dynamism of personal affection. So a Frenchman, Raoul de Roussy de Sales, said a generation ago, "America appears to be the only country in the world where love is a national problem." What Americans are trying to do, in other words, is to achieve what is almost an impossible task, one that most of the other cultures of the world never even attempted. They are trying to deepen their relationships, make the experience of intimacy more meaningful, and to stabilize, according to these high-order values, the man-woman relationship in marriage. There is little surprise, then, that the divorce rate is high in the United States. It is not because America is a nation falling apart or one filled with moral degenerates; it is because Americans seek a genuine experience of intimacy and count those relationships as superficial and unacceptable which do not provide them. They are searching for the right circumstances in which love and marriage can flourish side by side. There are not many other people in the world taking this problem seriously. Americans, however, are hardly conscious of what they are attempting to do because they are so conscious of the problems involved in trying to achieve it.

The possibilities, within the clumping machinery employed by the human condition to process deep insights, of working out a better relationship between man and woman are found in America at the present time. Although the discussions are beset with conflicts, poorly defined terms, and regular exchanges of hostility, Americans are fighting against the permanent institutionalization of inequity between the sexes. They are literally battling through the false positions and temporary peaces that have been forged in so many other cultures and lands and they show no signs of resting until something better than the double standard has been reached in the United States.

This means that the days of the he-man freak are numbered; his passing will not be a tragedy because he is the man, of all men, most vulnerable to the pressure to prove himself. The future offers the possibility that men will be able to understand themselves in richer and less restrictive terms than have been allowed to them in the great era of the hunter and the hero. Man may, as he gets what truly proves a man to be a man into clearer focus—and as we allow sex, breathless and worn-looking, to assume a more realistic role in life—find himself more sure of himself than he has been for a long time. The future's inevitable de-emphasis on genital sexuality will allow people to become more truly sexual in a more cooperative and less competitive way. The promise sown into the current American conflict is that we may find that, despite the lack of a cease-fire in the battle of the sexes, men and women are actually in the process of healing each other's wounds.

The key to this is their capacity to come out of this free of the notion that they need be identical while, at the same time, they have a deepened respect for the fact that, as human beings, they are truly equal. The dangerous over-generalization that flows from some of the discussions of the equality of women obliterates the genuine contrast and differences between the sexes which are so essential for a sound and self-confident realization of each of them. There is no question about the fact that equality has been denied to woman in many ways; to grant it to her does not make her the same as a man physiologically or psychologically; it makes her the same as a man as a person. It is, in fact, a long failure to recognize this fundamental equality that has led to so many of the other distortions, which we are only now beginning to correct. Out of the present ferment men and women may, in fact, step forward more equal and more different from each other at the same time.

It takes distance from the current scene to understand the rich possibilities of outcome that have been unrecognized and unverbalized by most observers until now. Most of the males have only followed out in their writings the intuition of the threat that many of them feel, and both men and women have confused equality with identity. Americans are pursuing a goal of great value both for themselves and for the rest of the world. It will not be easily achieved. Indeed, as has just been noted, it is almost impossible to place the goal of men and women as equal persons clearly into focus. There are, however, despite the prophets of gloom, reasons for optimism. American men and women are struggling together with a big issue—the man-woman issue—and they are taking it seriously. They are working toward the development of a deeper consciousness of themselves as persons and a keener awareness of the values that are essential for the full development of male and female human beings. This is not the kind of question that is of concern to people who are totally depraved. Americans are reaching for an ideal, as they have, in one way or another, throughout their history. They will clarify and dramatize essential aspects of a question that has been put off for centuries. If their eventual achievement is only partially successful, Americans will have seemed more honest than sophisticated, more hopeful than depraved. They may also make it possible for men and women to achieve deeper and better relationships in the generations ahead.

13
AN OLD-FASHIONED MYTH

Contemporary man has woven himself a threadbare coat of sexual myth and it has not comforted or kept him very warm against the savage winds of reality. Some prophets have tried to look beyond the edges of the present situation, past the shattered walls and thin columns of smoke that border man's sexual world. They project different pictures of the future but they do not necessarily provide clues to the basic problems at the heart of man's sexual confusion. A new world of even greater permissiveness is just over the horizon, according to some. Others see a diminution of the fascination with and concentration on genital sexuality; still other observers read the future as a bland and neutral environment inhabited by sexes that have gradually dissolved into one.

There is some truth in all these visions; they are extensions of trends which can already be observed in the present, although not in overwhelmingly clear form. These trends are not, however, anything dramatically new. They can be traced back to earlier times and other prophets; they have been on the world's radar screen for some time, and they have, in fact, been partially fulfilled in this century. Whether these trends are, however, strong enough to shape the thrust of culture in the future is debatable. These trends are signs of the deeper unresolved sexual difficulties of human beings; they are the future as an outgrowth of myth rather than of the ultimate possibilities of the human person. In other words, if the present illusions about sexuality persist, man's sexual adjustment in the next generation will necessarily be an extension of his present focus. He will pursue the mythic goals which even now constitute a source of frustration for him. This will lead, painfully but surely, to a world in which monogamy will be remembered more than practiced. So, too, the intense glare of the current floodlit concentration on genital sexuality will inevitably cause a certain blindness in the onlookers as, incompletely rewarded for all their earnest examination of this part of human sexuality, they search out a broader perspective from which to view sex in the human condition. In the same way, the signs of threat and uneasiness between the sexes may well lead more people to settle for a muting of their sexual instincts in an effort to minimize interpersonal friction through a lessening of the contrasts between men and women. The scenario for this has already been written; it is being acted out in hundreds of settings already. These various futures are, however, not visions of sexual redemption as much as they are the logical development of a culture that follows myths rather than maps of reality into tomorrow.

To continue the oversimplification that is necessary in a work of this size, disintegrated sex necessarily breeds a second-generation strain of more disintegrated sex. As has been noted earlier, when the fundamental problem may be defined as man's inability to get himself completely together, then he is not helped by solutions which only tear him more apart. The present mythology, distorting both sexual knowledge and personality theory, forces sexuality out of proper focus, giving it a false sense of independent existence under a hundred liberated aliases. But, smooth as the rationalizations sound, sex that is pried away from the person leaves a wound that may be bandaged but never healed by myth. Freedom is a word with no substantive meaning in the mythical pathways dug, like unalterable trenches, in the landscape of human experience.

It has never been enough just to give man information

or more detailed instructions about how to operate certain aspects of his physiological mechanism. Man cries out to be treated like a human being rather than a machine. He is not mechanical, and in the long run, he will reject the schemes which treat him so. His basic problem, the one that runs a ground swell under the myths that try to fence him in, is that he is seeking experience that is richer and deeper than that which can be provided by philosophies of pleasure or economies of affluence. Man searches for a proper sense of himself and he moves instinctively toward those human experiences which can provide this. Beneath all the stage apparatus of the sexual revolution, man is seeking some humanly validating communion with other persons; he longs, in other words, for the deep kind of intimacy through which he truly experiences himself as man. The signs of sexual preoccupation and experimentation merely illustrate the human existential dilemma—the search for meaning, personal and communal, through sexual experience which is keyed to deeper realities—in a world that cannot get beneath the erotic surface of sex as it lives by myth rather than reality.

Contemporary man's problems with sexuality cannot really be defined as sexual problems. This is to compound the distortions which have already made man nearsighted in this area. Just as the person is more than sexual, so his problems transcend the sexual as well. Our chronic inability to keep this truth in mind has led to much of the confusion over programs that have been designed to help man understand his sexuality. Sexual information is not enough, as reliable authorities in the field of sex education have tried to say as clearly as possible for years. It is indeed curious that something as important and needed as sex education has become the center of so much stormy controversy. That is another kind of sign, of course, a sign of man's defensiveness about sex that emerges in his conflicted attitudes toward dispelling the miasma of myth and ignorance that have done him so much harm. One would expect a reasonable, if moderate amount of enthusiasm, for such worthy projects. Instead, most sex-education programs, even those endorsed by respected religious and educational leaders, are the subject of strong positive and negative feelings. The salvationists see sex education as the answer to all the difficulties of the next generation; their bright faith is undimmed even when the programs are poorly carried out by unqualified personnel. Far worse are the paranoid reactions of those who interpret sex-education courses as subversive activities, plots to muddle American minds and weaken the American will to resist communism or some other plot. There is, then, a special fierce mythology connected with sex education, one which in its own way reflects the primal dual myth that the world is about to experience either a new golden dawn or a final blackened night. The sex-education issue is like a screen onto which the myth machine projects the fears and uncertainties of many Americans. This basically sound movement has thus been twisted into being part of the problem rather than part of the solution.

Ultimately, as with so many other deeply disturbing contemporary issues, the problem is fundamentally a religious one. This will seem an outrageous assertion to many people, especially to those who think that the churches have contributed a great deal to creating the present painful situation. Another camp will hold, of course, that the Church should return to its role as the custodian of purity and leave sex, like politics, alone. There is no point in denying the fact that religious institutions, for complicated reasons, coupled sex with sin and virtue with absolute purity at certain points in history. The Christian churches, insofar as they have been guilty of this, certainly contributed to the disintegration of sex from personality, the original sin, in a sense, that has spawned the myths of our modern-day confusion. It is, however, a myth to identify all religion as blind and repressive of the human spirit. Only men are blind and repressive and many of these, their energies compressed like those of the Apollo engines, have shaped religious institutions in the image of their own fears. Some of the churchmen most estranged

from the Christian vision of man have had the most powerful effect in institutionalizing a Christian prejudice against
sex. To say that churchmen have made mistakes is to acknowledge of them what must be admitted about every
other group of men. It is also to distinguish what is truly
religious from the distorted interpretations men have given
it over the years. Religion is only now straightening out
its own mythology; the Christian Gospels, purged of a
magical overlay, are being read again as compelling challenges to the full humanization of man. The most significant recent shift of theological mood has been the shift
from a world-negating to a world-affirming attitude. The
Gospels, read now in their original bold simplicity, are seen
to challenge man to find and fulfill his human promise
even at the price of suffering and death. Religion has once
again focused itself on human experience rather than on
heavenly goals. The developments in theology have placed
man and his growth at the center of concern once more.
Indeed, many false and inadequate religious visions have
collapsed in this century; most of these were built on elementary notions of faith, notions that are no longer accepted in a better educated world. Religious faith emerges
now as an encompassing way of life rather than as a rit-
ualistic manipulation of fears or a commitment to certain
unalterable semantics of dogma. Religion is recovering
slowly from its neurotic illness, and although the development is far from complete, it is relinquishing its controlling authoritarian style for one that encourages and vali-
dates man's strength to respond to the spirit in an
atmosphere of freedom. Organized religion has lost its influence precisely to the extent that it has insisted on a
common-denominator type of faith preached in an un-
yielding authoritarian manner. But the power of the
Gospels, even independent of creaking religious institutions, has attracted the imagination and touched the con-
sciences of persons everywhere. Religion has come to deal
once more with the most paramount of issues: How will
we live as responsible and free human beings? This is a
question asked recurrently by serious men in every part

of the world. Mihajlo Mihajlov, the Yugoslav writer and philosopher, put it this way:

> Why delude ourselves? Freedom of men and society is not a scientific-technical problem but an existential one. That means first of all a religious problem. (The New York *Times,* July 26, 1971, p. 25.)

Religion, its institutional managers shrinking back for fear that their influence is waning, is actually being challenged once more to deal not with the accidentals of piety but with the essentials of life. Only a religious response is adequate to make sense of the jumble of problems—political, educational, technological, and personal—which have piled up on man's doorstep like the uncollected residue of history. Religion's perennial task has not been to intimidate or to control man but to free him for life through lighting up its meaning for him. The persistence of sexual mythology illustrates the inability of technological or informational responses to clarify completely man's understanding of his sexuality. Religion, of all the forces we know, clearly possesses the power and the schemas of ultimate interpretation which can answer the questions that come from the hearts of searching man. The sexual difficulties of twentieth-century man are too profoundly human to be other than religious issues.

The assertion does not mean, of course, that the churches are prepared to join themselves to man's struggle for sexual understanding. Many of them are, however, trying to do this, and although their progress is slow, they are making some headway. The problem for organized religions is, of course, to transform themselves from agencies with all the answers to those which are willing to ask the most difficult of questions about how we should live. The late Bishop Pike had a hold on the essence of the challenge; man needs more belief and fewer beliefs. He will be redeemed sexually only as he is redeemed humanly. The integration of his sexuality will only be achieved when he can integrate himself into the larger context of life and meaning that enables him to see all of reality rather than very narrow samples of it. Religion must obviously affirm the worth of man and the value of his struggle for wholeness. It must put aside its human urge to censor and supervise man for a more spiritual role of freeing man to explore and truly find himself. The churches will not be able to give a wholehearted religious response to man's sexual problems until they have truly validated rather than just tolerated the essential sexuality of the person. Religion can give meaning in a compassionate and sensitive manner, but only after it has come to terms with its own sexuality. It is time for religious leaders to sense religion's present opportunity to serve growing man by purging itself of its own throat-clearing uneasiness about sex so that it can truly share the Gospel values whose power to integrate human personality remains vigorous despite the calamitous blunders of organized religion. When the churches demonstrate that they can deal responsibly with man's sexuality they will also have demonstrated that they have gotten religion again. Until religious institutions perceive human sexuality as a broad religious issue rather than just a moral one, man will continue to invent new versions of old myths to comfort himself against the jagged edges of his own ignorance.

The mythology of sex, that recurrent haze that obstructs man's vision of himself, is a mechanism of adjustment employed for lack of a more unifying and satisfying theology of life. Religion that has itself in perspective can assist man to place sex into a perspective of human meaning; faith that is adult can still make man whole. Unless the churches realize that man's sexual dilemmas are their urgent concern, the outcomes forecast by various prophets are bound to occur. The ultimate sin may be the failure to respond to man who, in so many ways, is signaling that he needs to discover a sense of his own significance once more. He is looking for the right kind of myth—the one that conveys ageless meaning in terms of rich human experience—the kind of myth that is the most religious of all.